FRESH BREAD FROM HEAVENS BAKERY

"FOR IF YOU ONLY KNEW THAT HEAVENS BREAD WILL BRING YOU OUT OF CAPITIVITY"

By TERRY YOUNG

Fresh Bread From Heavens Bakery by Terry Young
Published by Terry Young
Printed by Terry Young
Riverside, Ca. 92509
E-Mail: terry1@aceweb.com
www.driminc.org
www.theorygiftbaskets.com

This book or parts therefore may not be reproduced in any form, stored in a retrieval system, or transmitted in any form by any means-electronic, mechanical, photocopy, recording, or otherwise-without prior written permission of the publisher, except as provided by the United States of America copy right law.

Unless otherwise noted, all Scripture quotations are from the King James Version of the Bible.
Copyright© 1979, 1980, 1982 by Thomas Nelson Inc, Used with permission. All rights reserved
Scripture quotations marked AMP are from the Amplified Bible. Old Testament copyright©1965 1987 Zondervan Corporation. The Amplified New Testament copyright©1954 1958, 1962, 1964, 1965, 1987 Lockman Foundation. Used by permission.
Design Director: Terry Young
Cover Designer: Terry Young
Copyright© 2010 by Terry Young
(Dorothy Ray International Ministries, Inc.)
Riverside, California. 92517-1458
All rights reserved
For more information about this book, send inquires to
draymin@aceweb.com
terry1@aceweb.com
theorygiftbaskets@yahoo.com

ISBN # 0-9777333-1-9
ISBN # 978-0-9777333-16

Table Of Contents

Table Of Contents.. 3

Forward.. 4

Introduction... 5

Chapter 1: Knowledge.. 7

Chapter 2: What Does The Word Of God Say About Tithing.... 13

Chapter 3: Tithing Is One Of The Requirements For Walking In Your Inheritance.. 26

Chapter 4: Tithe Is The First Tenth................................ 37

Chapter 5: Tithing Or Tipping...................................... 42

Chapter 6: Law Of Nature.. 60

Chapter 7: Obedience In Giving.................................. 76

Chapter 8: Elijah The Tishbite..................................... 86

Chapter 9: God's Reward System................................. 89

Chapter 10: A Seed Sown In Faith Will Meet Any Need......... 107

Chapter 11: Claming Your Rights as An Heir Of God............ 123

Chapter 12: The Woman With The Alabaster Box Who Washed Jesus Feet With Her Tears................... 128

Chapter 13: Whatever You Can See By Faith You Can Have.... 136

Chapter 14: You And God Make An Unbeatable Team.......... 148

Prayer For Money To Come In..................................... 155

Forward

I met Terry Young in 1986 at a church in Riverside. We were in an evangelism program. Every Sunday evening the custom was to send two people out to minister to new people who came to the church.

We went to minister at a home and when we came out of their home, we saw a bright white cloud over the driveway. Terry said, "What's that?" And I said, "It's a cloud of glory." We stood there for about a half an hour watching God change the pictures in the cloud.

Since that time, Terry and his wife, Margaret, and I have worked together in the ministry.

Terry is an elder, minister of the gospel, has the call of pastor on his life, and he is also a computer expert. He created my website, book covers for my books, live internet streaming, and on, and on.

He is dedicated to serving God with all his life.

God has given him knowledge about the use of money for the Kingdom of God.

This book will bless you and open your eyes to many true stories about the correct use of money in order to get the wealth of the wicked into your hands in this end time.

Dorothy Ray
Dorothy Ray International Ministry

Introduction

Here is the Scenario: You hear the siren

An Announcement takes place in heaven, there has been a robbery.

Angels are dispatched. The reply comes back! We caught Him. Then take him before the Lord.

The Lord says you have done a two fold robbery.

You ask: Where in have I robbed you?

The Lord replies:

Your first robbery is in your tithes
Your second robbery is in your offerings
Mal 3:8

The verdict:
You are guilty.

The Sentence:
I allow the devourer to bring destruction and famine in your life

I will give you a way out:
Repent
For with holding of your tithes I sentence a Fifth (20% late fee on you)
Lev 17:21

It is important to reiterate that God blesses us so we can support his kingdom.
God reigns and rules over this earth.
He promotes his eternal plan.

God put money in the children of Israel's hands.
He couldn't ask them for an offering unless He provided something for them to give.
It's the same today.
He puts money in our hands then he asks us for not only our tithes, but for an offering as well.
Our tithes and offerings bless his work.
When we bless his work, we can't help but be blessed.

Remember Knowledge is power:
Hosea 4:6 says My people are destroyed for lack of knowledge: because thou hast rejected knowledge, I will also reject thee, that thou shalt be no priest to me: seeing thou hast forgotten the law of thy God, I will also forget thy children.

So the cause of man's problem is lack of knowledge (information; God's Word), but there is no shortage of information (God's Word), rather a rejection of information (God's Word). I'm telling you we have really missed it and believed so many lies, that the adversary, the enemy is having a field day with us. Have you heard this said (What I don't know won't hurt me) Well what a lie. What you don't know is killing you. Example: If you are sick and don't know what to do it may kill you, but with the right knowledge you can live.

Now let's go one step deeper

Isaiah 5:13 says Therefore my people are gone into captivity, because they have no knowledge: and their honorable men are famished, and their multitude dried up with thirst. So again the question is: What is holding you in captivity, Fear, Sickness, Lack not knowing who you are? Not knowing what the Word of God reveals about your condition (mind set).Well my friend the Word of God can set you free.

CHAPTER 1

Knowledge

Statement: No Financial Institution or Banking Company collects funds public or private, gives out an increase with out a deposit or investment being made. Any interest paid out is only on the amount of money invested into that account. No matter how high the interest rate at a lending institution may be, that institution will pay no increase unless there has been a deposit made.

Most savings plans in banks only give; if your lucky 2- 4% a year. The larger the amount you deposit, will cause them to give you a little more 6%-8%, and maybe that new toaster, but guess what they have restrictions such as minimum deposits, lengthy time of deposit, and substantial penalties for any deviation (early withdrawal). Now what you are doing is loaning the bank your money for 2%-8% and they are using your money to invest at a higher rate of return to them.

But thank God that when you give into the kingdom of God He is generous; that is the condition. You must make a deposit

Let's give you some more information
There is a rule of 72 you may or may not know about.
Very simply stated: If you were to invest $100.00 with compounding interest at a rate of 9% per annum, the rule of 72 (9% divided into 72 = 8 years) which is required for your investment to be worth $200.00. What if you were to be able to invest like your credit cards 19% or higher. No wonder they want you to stay in debt with your credit card.

Let's give you some food for thought

God had scientific facts to be recorded in the Bible long before scientists discovered them. Here are just a couple, and I'm sure you can think of many more.

How is the earth held in place?   Job 26:7(AMP) He it is Who spreads out the northern skies over emptiness and hangs the earth upon or over nothing.

How deep is the ocean? In the 1900's oceanographers found the sea has many deep valleys or canyons, and the deepest canyons are called trenches. The Marianas Trench in the Pacific is so deep that if you could drop Mt. Everest which is 29,000' High) into it, it's peak would be 1 mile below the waters surface. The Atlantic Ocean has an under water mountain range 10,000 miles long. Jonah 2:6(AMP) says I went down to the bottoms and the very roots of the mountains; the earth with its bars closed behind me forever. Yet You have brought up my life from the pit and corruption, O Lord my God.

How come an apple falls to the ground instead of falling upward

Knowledge is what Mark Zuckerberg used to create Face Book and at the age of 23 his annual turnover is $700 Million Dollars

Knowledge is what Blake Ross and David Hyatt used to create Mozilla and at the age of 22 their annual turnover is $120 Million Dollars.

Knowledge is what Chad Hurley used to create Youtube and at the age of 30 his annual turnover is $85 Million Dollars and so goes the list.

Knowledge today is at the forefront of everything good and bad. But the knowledge that will benefit mankind is the word of God.

Knowledge just as the increase of the agricultural harvest demands that a seed must be planted, so the increase of your finances demands that some of your finances must be planted (tithed).

This knowledge from God's word is called the Law of Seed Time and Harvest (more on this in chapter 2).

Father God established the law of seed time and harvest, because God sowed His son Jesus in the earth

Example of this is found in John 12:24 says except a corn of wheat fall into the ground and die, it abideth alone; but if it die, it bringeth forth much fruit. What this means is…Our financial seed when it is sown into the work of the Lord, it must cease to benefit us. It must be released totally into the hands and control of those who preach the Gospel.

Statement: When it comes to money we have a hard time believing God is our supply.

When your mind is divided between God on one hand and earthly riches on the other, your faith wavers and you become double minded, and in James 1:8(AMP) which says (For being as he is) a man of two minds (hesitating, dubious, irresolute), (he is) unstable and unreliable and uncertain about everything (he thinks, feels, decides). A double vision interferes with a right relationship with God, who wants to be our sole source of supply (Philippians 4:19)

The word in (John 3:30) says God must increase and we must decrease. He has a higher calling for us; to have our minds reprogrammed to contain his mind. We need to get set free from the poverty mentality. Always confessing what we don't have. We need to see our-self the way God sees us in 3 John 2. That means we must release all our cares to Jesus as our I 'am (whatever we have need of in our time of need) our provider, our healer, our nourisher, our banner.

Money represents a portion of our very lives, we put time in on a job and in return for that time, we are compensated wages. This is where our attitude check needs to take place. So the question again is our security and faith in the people, place, or things, including money?

1 Timothy 6:10: says the love of money is the root of all evil... It is not Money is the root of all-evil. I believe that God loves us so much that he will go to great lengths to see to it that we can never find complete contentment with the things of this world.

Truth: You are only a steward, (defined as a person who manages another's property or finances) never an owner, of all things that the Lord has entrusted to our care, including money. You should believe that God is your whole source.

You can make wrong decisions by trusting in people rather than the Lord about your finances and other matters that will open you up to bitterness; (Which we can define as Unforgiveness) so you need to change your mind by trusting in the Lord.

Also if you have a critical spirit, which opens the door for envy and jealousy and brings you into unbelief that God will not supply all your needs.

The word in (John 3:30) says God must increase and we must decrease. He has a higher calling for us; to have our minds reprogrammed to have a Christ like mind.

So now you ask, Just how do I do get a Christ like mind?
The word of God says in (Romans 12:2) And be not conformed to this world: but be ye transformed by the renewing of your mind, that ye may prove what is that good, and acceptable, and perfect, will of God.

2 Timothy 2:25: Paul say's, "Those who oppose him he must gently instruct, in the hope that God will grant them repentance leading them to a knowledge of the truth, and that they will come to their senses and escape from the trap of the devil, who has taken them captive to do his will".

Romans 10:17(AMP) says So faith comes by hearing (what is told), and what is heard comes by the preaching (of the message that came from the lips) of Christ (the Messiah Himself)

You won't do what God says in His Word if your mind is not renewed daily with the Word of God, for you will only receive what you believe, and you will only believe what you receive. In other words, why would you give of your money or anything else if you don't believe that God is real and that He is not a man that He would lie. If God is your source of supply then you will have no problem with (Luke 6:30,34,35)

"Give to every man that asketh of thee, that wants necessaries, which thou hast wherewithal to supply out of thy superfluities. Give to those that are not able to help themselves." And if you lend to those from whom you expect repayment, what credit is that to you? Even sinners lend to sinners, expecting to be repaid in full. But love your enemies, do good to them, and lend to them without expecting to get anything back. Then your reward will be great Luke 6:30,34,35.

What ever you need, begin to encourage yourself in the word and ask the Holy Spirit to help you, whether it be for healing, finances or deliverance. Use God's word the way He intended, by speaking it out of your mouth, for His word will defeat the giants in your life. We have to have knowledge according to 2 Corinthians 2:11 Lest Satan should get an advantage of us: for we are not ignorant of his devices.

Pray this out loud:

We bind our money (finances) to the will of God and loose the deception of poverty, lack, worry, and fear of not having what we want or need to live on this earth. We tear apart, crush, wreck and pull asunder every plot and plan of the enemy to keep us, our families, homes, jobs, and ministry from having our needs met. We pull down every stronghold that would keep us from receiving what the word says is ours. "Our God said he would supply all our need according to his riches in glory by Christ Jesus."

CHAPTER 2

What Does The Word Of God Say About Tithing

Abraham believed in one true God.
He believed that his God would deliver him from the hands of his enemies-and he proved it.

Gen: 14, tells us about Abraham's nephew Lot and his family, who lived in the wicked city of Sodom, that they were captured and carried off by an enemy army. Let me inject this, our belief in God teaches us to be for peace, yet it does not forbid us to provide for war.

Abraham didn't agree with Lot's life style in Sodom. Now get this, because he was a righteous man, Abraham wanted to rescue his kinsman. He gathered his 318 men and pursued this enemy army, though it was much larger in number, and brought back his loved ones, plus all the loot that had been taken.

So Abraham returned in victory, and was met by the high priest, Melchizedek. Now the word says his success was very considerable that He defeated his enemies, and rescued his friends; and did not sustain any loss. Gen 14:18-20 gives and account that Melchizedek king of Salem and priest of the Most High (king of righteousness and king of peace).

Melchizedek, the priest of God, came out to greet Abraham. He brought forth bread and wine, for the refreshment of Abram and his soldiers, and in congratulation of their victory. This he did as a king. When he saw Abraham, GET THIS praise broke forth on his lips. He said in verse 19, 20 blessed be Abraham of the most high God, possessor of heaven and earth:

And blessed be the most high God, which hath delivered thine enemies into thy hand. This he did as priest of the most high God,

After this blessing, Abraham did a remarkable thing-something nobody had ever done before. AND HE GAVE HIM TITHES OF ALL. Not just a tithe of his money, but a tithe of all that he owned.

Revelation:
Abraham blessed, praised, and glorified God Most High because he realized God as possessor and maker of heaven and earth, who had given his foes into his hand, and then honored him by giving him a tenth of all (he had taken).

We, who are of the faith of Abraham, need to come to know what Abraham knew as he gave those tithes and offerings to the Lord.
Abraham recognized the three most important things about God:
1. The Lord is the most high God
2. He is the possessor of heaven and earth
3. He is the deliverer from all our enemies.

Revelation;
Abraham gave these tithes to God over 400 years before Moses received the Law.
Tithing was not instituted by the Mosaic Law. Tithing became a part of the Law of Moses through the understanding that they were to believe God as the most high God, possessor of heaven and earth, and deliverer from all enemies. Because God was all these things to them, they gave tithes and offerings to Him. Tithing was a creative part of their overall faith in who God was and who they were as God's people.

Promise: Since we are seed's of Abraham, we can accept that same blessing and see God just as Abraham saw him at that moment.

Now in verse 21,22. The King of Sodom approached him and pointed to all the loot. The King said, "Give me the persons, and take the goods to thyself".

Abraham's response to the offer of the King of Sodom
Abraham said (now wait a minute king old buddy) to the King of Sodom, I have lift up mine hand unto the Lord, the most high God, the possessor of heaven and earth, That I will not take from a thread even to a shoe latchet, and that I will not take any thing that is thine, lest thou shouldest say, I have made Abraham rich. Abraham gave tithes of all and put his trust only in God. God was Abraham's source, and he refused to accept anything from that man. He declared to the King of Sodom: "God will make me rich, not you"!

Abraham knew his tithes were seed from which God would bless him and supply all his needs.
Then when he was old and ready to die, it was written of him. Now you know he must have been old because the bible records it. And Abraham was old, and well stricken in age: and the Lord had blessed Abraham in all things.
Key: If you do not know Who God is, you will never know who you are. And you will never give your tithes to the Lord as Abraham did.

The King of Sodom tried to buy him off, but Abraham refused adamantly, saying: My God is most high. He owns everything! My God owns it all! Why should I stoop to take a shoelace? Then you could brag and say, "Look what I did for Abraham!"

1. "No king" My God will make me rich. You're no source to me. My God is my Source!

2. My God is higher than you. He is higher than your god. Your god couldn't even keep you from being captured.

3. My God not only kept me from being captured, He gave me power to rescue you. He gave me power to rescue your people.

He gave me power to rescue my nephew and his family, and bring back all that was taken.

4. My God delivered me from all my enemies. He is most high. He owns it all; and because I worship and give tithes to Him as my source, He will make me richer than you can. It is God Who gives power to get wealth because only God owns the wealth of the world.

Abraham believed God. He became a man of faith, the miracle-working kind of faith that enabled him to live the fullest life of all.
Abraham was 100 years old and Sarah, his wife, was 90 when God spoke to him and told him that they would bare a child.
Abraham believed what God told him. He believed this incredible promise because his worship of God and his giving tithes to God were in the rhythm of faith. His seed-faith was being constantly planted to God. Miraculously, Sarah conceived and bore a son, Isaac.

That miracle birth was the beginning of the people who would come to be known through the world as God's chosen People. People who, as children of Abraham, believed God was the most high God, possessor of heaven and earth, deliverer from all their enemies, and multiplier of their tithes given to Him to meet their needs.

Abraham begat Isaac, the son of promise
Isaac begat Jacob (later his name was changed to Israel because he chose to stop living by his wits and start trusting God as his source).

Jacob or Israel bore 12 sons whose descendants came to be known as the twelve tribes of Israel.
Their descendants became the children of Israel, and from them came our Savior, Jesus Christ, Whom Saint Paul calls the Son of David (Romans 1:3)

This is how the seed faith principle brought our Savior Jesus into the world.

We must come to understand who God is.
God is the most high, the possessor of the heavens and the earth, the deliverer from your enemies. We must know God as our source and total supply.

To reach a place that you give tithes joyously of all you have. As you do these things, God's blessing will be upon you as it was with Abraham and you will become so prosperous, so blessed, so anointed of God that you will conquer everything before you. As long as you look to God as your source, you cannot be defeated. In being blessed you will become a blessing to all people. If you are barely getting by, how could you be a blessing to others and how could you know God as your source and how could you tell others how great God is.

The doctrine of tithing is also found in Matthew 23:23: Woe to you scribes and Pharisees, pretenders-hypocrites! (Jesus is saying in this, that you love the best seats in the synagogues and greetings in the market place).
Let me define a Pharisee: Members of one of the three major parties in Judaism that emphasized strict interpretation and observance of the Mosaic law a hypocritical self righteous one. Jesus was closer to this group than to any other, as indicated by his comments about them. For you give a tenth of mint and dill and cumin, and have neglected and omitted the weightier (more important) matters of the law, right and justice and mercy, and fidelity. These you ought (particularly) to have done, without neglecting the others.

And on the other hand, in his Sermon on the Mount he said "For I say to you, that unless your righteousness exceeds the righteousness of the scribes and Pharisees, you will by no means enter the Kingdom of Heaven" Matthew 5:20

Leviticus 27:30 And all the tithe of the land, whether of the seed of the land or of the fruit tree, is the Lord's; it is holy to the Lord.

History: Several species of mint grow in Palestine. Anise is better rendered dill and it grew both wild and cultivated, its fruits being used for medicine. The seeds of cumin, which resemble caraway, were used as spice in seasoning. In such little matters the Pharisees were most careful to keep the law, yet they had completely overlooked its more important precepts. (Judgment mercy and faith).

Malachi 3:8-11: Will a man rob or defraud God? Yet you rob and defraud Me. But you say, In what way do we rob or defraud You? You have withheld your tithes and offerings,

9. You are cursed with the curse; for you are robbing Me, even this whole nation. (AMP)

10. Bring all the tithes-the whole tenth of your income- into the storehouse, that there may be food in My house, and prove Me now by it, says the Lord of Hosts, if I will not open the windows of Heaven for you and pour you out a blessing, that there shall not be room enough to receive it. (AMP)

11. And I will rebuke the devourer (insects and plagues) for your sakes, and he shall not destroy the fruits of your ground; neither shall your vine drop its fruit before the time in the field says the Lord of hosts. (AMP)

Proverbs 3:9-10 Honor the Lord with thy substance, and with the first fruits of all thine increase.
10. So shall thy barns be filled with plenty, and thy presses shall burst out with new wine. Barns are talking about a place where you put your money. God is saying if a person will honor him, He will see to it that he doesn't go broke! God is saying to the one who honors Him, "I am the Lord thy God. I am Jehovah Jireh. I am the Lord who provides".

Deut 8:18 But thou shalt remember the Lord thy God: for it is he that giveth thee POWER to get wealth, that he may establish his covenant which he sware unto thy fathers, as it is this day.

God will see to it that if you handle the seed and the power properly, you will have the increase. You need to recognize that God has given us everything we need to be prosperous. But the problem is the body of Christ has not known how to use the tools the father has provided for them to attain financial stability and prosperity even as 3 John 2 says.

God has given us seed, power, and increase. God is saying, "Listen my children, money is no problem; the silver and gold is Mine. I'll give you the seed to plant, the power to get wealth". (Deuteronomy 8:18AMP) which says; But you shall (earnestly) remember the Lord your God, for it is he Who gives you power to get wealth, that He may establish His covenant which He swore to your fathers, as it is this day and the increase to cause it to come to pass in your life, but the seed, power and increase won't work, if you don't let me know what your going to do with the prosperity when you get it.

Isaiah 55:10,11 (AMP) For as the rain and snow come down from the heavens, and return not there again, but water the earth and make it bring forth and sprout, that it may give seed to the sower and bread to the eater.

11. So shall My word be that goes forth out of My mouth; it shall not return void-without producing any effect, useless - but it shall accomplish that which I please and purpose, and it shall prosper in the things for which I sent it.

Faith tells us that the problem is the 12 x 12 block on our shoulders, (our head) that encourages us to say to the Lord (if I see it I will believe it).The Lord says if you believe it, then you will see it. (Real Faith Always Turns To Sight). You see you have to get out of the natural and walk by faith, not by sight, concerning the things God has promised us in His Word. I have Planted, Apollos watered; but God gave the increase.
(1 Corinthians:3:6)

The Lord wants to establish a money covenant with the believers such as only a few have experienced until now.
But it takes the Bible information to change a person's situation. It's called renew your mind with the Word of God. We must be confident in the Word of God and convinced of the will of God, so we might say that God meets my every need and I have an abundant supply.

Psalm 35:27   Let them shout for joy, and be glad, that favor my righteous cause: yea, let them say continually, let the Lord be magnified, which hath pleasure in the prosperity of his servant.

God does not want you to barely get by, so don't accept barely getting by, it's a lie. You've got to speak out of your mouth what God says in His word. Don't sit around and say nothing, speak out the word of God. Say what God says about you (I'm highly favored, created for greatness. I shall not want or lack any good thing).

In prospering us, God is only doing what He wants to do for his children. He has been saying it down thru the ages. God wants us out of debt. He wants us out of distress and He wants us out of discouragement. And the only way that can happen is by our prospering as 3 John 2 says. Beloved , I wish above all things that thou mayest prosper and be in health, even as thy soul prospereth, that means Physically, Mentally, Financially, Spiritually, in other words totally.

Prosperity begins with Obedience, Deuteronomy 8:1   All the commandments which I command thee this day shall ye observe to do, that ye may live, and multiply, and go in and possess the land which I sware unto your fathers. This gives us some specific direction for being in the will of God. All the commandments which I command thee this day shall ye observe to do. So you have to be A DOER OF GOD'S COMMANDMENTS TO RECEIVE GOD'S BLESSINGS. There is no short cut or side door to get in on God's blessings, you can't slide in or creep in a side door by prayer when God told you to give. You can't pray past giving!

The Bible says that the prayer of a righteous man availeth much (James 5:16). So then the question becomes? What is a righteous man? I'm so glad you asked and now I will tell you. A righteous man is one who favors God's righteous cause. In other words, God blesses those who do what He tells them to do. We as children of God are supposed to be controlling this financial system instead of this financial system controlling us!

The reason people are so money minded is because they don't have money, and they have to think about where they are going to get money from! But those who have money don't even think about it. Lets face it, if you had all the money you needed, you would think about something else like maybe Love, if that was what you lacked.

What has God said about prosperity?
Do you believe God and what He has said in His Word?
Do you believe that God is not a liar?
Do you believe that what He said in His Word, He meant for all us to have?

Well in Psalm 35:27   Let them shout for joy, and be glad, that favor my righteous cause: yea, let them say continually, Let the Lord be magnified, which hath pleasure in the prosperity of his servant.

When you're in God's divine program financially, it brings joy and gladness! You have to cleanse your mind of wrong, messed up thinking concerning money. The Bible says we're cleansed through the word. John 15:3

If ye then, being evil (or natural), know how to give good gift's unto your children, how much more shall your Father which is in heaven give good things to them that ask Him?
(Matthew 7:11).

Give, and it shall be given you; good measure, pressed down, and shaken together, and running over, shall men give into your bosom. For with the same measure that you mete withal it shall be measured to you again. Luke 6:38: good measure, pressed down and shaken together. It's part of the blood covenant. One of the reasons Jesus shed His Blood was so that we could have good measure. Good measure is when the basket is full. Deuteronomy 28:5

Pressed down means that when you press something down and you want to add some more to it, you shake the basket a little so that if there's any little crack that's not full, the contents will get into that crack.

Failing to tithe will cause money not to come to you. Haggai 1:6 Ye have sown much, and bring in little. That can never happen with God! It is impossible for you to sow much into the kingdom of God and come up with only a little. Luke 6:38 tells us why.

We need to remember whose we are and what our authority is in Jesus Christ, and get in line with God's Word.
We need to renew our mind daily with the Word
We need to keep a right attitude
We need to say what God says about us
We need to expand our vision about prosperity
We need to plead the blood over our finances
We need to shout for Joy and be Glad
We need to magnify the Lord, which hath pleasure in the prosperity of his servant.

Build a foundation with this
2 Chronicles 7:14-16 If My people who are called by My name shall humble themselves, pray, seek, crave and require of necessity My face, and turn from their wicked ways, then will (Then) I hear from heaven …..
(And) He will forgive our sin
(And) Heal our land.

In verse 15 (Now) My eyes will be open, (and) My ears attentive to prayer offered in this place
In verse 16 (For) I have chosen and sanctified (set apart for holy use) this house, that my name may be here for ever, (And) My eyes (and) My heart will be here perpetually.

This promise was originally given to Solomon regarding the people of Israel, but it applies to all who call on the Lord in repentance and faith. It stands as a high expression of God's loving readiness to hear the prayers of a repentant people.

Now I want to go back to what Abraham realized
(Discussed In Chapter 2)
He said in Gen14: verse 19-20: Blessed be Abraham of the most high God, possessor of heaven and earth:
And blessed be the most high God, which hath delivered thine enemies into thy hand.

After this blessing, Abraham did a remarkable thing-something nobody had ever done before. AND HE GAVE HIM TITHES OF ALL not just a tithe of his money, but a tithe of all that he owned.

Revelation:
Abraham blessed, praised, and glorified God Most High because he realized God as possessor and maker of heaven and earth, who had given his foes into his hand, and then honored him by giving him a tenth of all (he had taken).

Now he had the revelation of wholeness, fullness, and wellness which came through the revelation of SHALOM peace.
Colossians 3:15: And let the peace of God rule in your hearts.
Revelation: You cannot know wholeness, fullness, wellness without the revelation of the name JEHOVAH. SHALOM, is found only in peace which comes from YHUW.
The Lord (YAHWEH / JEHOVAH)

The Jews thought this name was to holy to pronounce, so they took the vowels from the Hebrew name Adonai (Lord) and inserted them in the name YHWH to make YAHOVAH (Jehovah). It's a combination of the Hebrew names for "GOD and LORD" and we might say Lord God.
Sanctification: Once you know the peace that surpasses all understanding then you will walk in the revelation (The Lord our Righteousness) In Jeremiah 23:5,6

Isa 45:25 you will be justified and enjoy righteousness, salvation and victory
Revelation:

In Elohim	He Created
In Jehovah	He Reveals
In Shaddai	He Supplies
In Adoni	He Purchased
In Jireh	He Redeems (provides)
In Rohi	He Heals (Jehova Repheka)
In Maccaddeshocn	He Sanctifies
In Shalom	He Fills
In Tsidkenu	He Makes Righteous

In Ps 23: The Lord is my Sheppard   Jehovah Rohi
In Isa 40:11: They had an intimacy with Jehovah
In Ezekiel 48:35: He revealed to Ezekiel. The Lord is there
As we begin to realize how great our source is,
We begin to have a revelation of God, (The Lord Yahweh/Jehovah).
That he is the God who always is
That He is the Self-Sufficient God
That He is the real God
That He is the Unchangeable God
That he is the Self-Fulfilled God
That the Lord is God (Jehovah-Elohim)
That He is a God worthy of worship
That He is the Lord God Most High (Jehovah-Elyon)
That He is The possessor of Heaven and Earth
That He is the Deliverer

That He is The Almighty God (El-Shaddai),
That He is The Lord will Provider (Jehovah-Jired),
That He is The Lord Is Healer (Jehovah-Repheka),
That He is The Lord Our Righteouness (Jehovah-Tsidqenu),

That He is The Lord Conqueror (Jehovah-Nissi),
That He is The Lord is Peace (Jehovah-Shalom),
That He is The Lord Is There (Jehovah-Shamah)

Let's pray this out loud…I bind all poverty and lack and I loose money and abundance of financial prosperity in my life and all those I lift up by name. Poverty will no longer control me or my family in money matters. Poverty will not cause us to become fearful of loss of money or lack of money. We will walk in prosperity and abundance of money in Jesus' name.

CHAPTER 3

Tithing Is One Of The Requirements For Walking In Your Inheritance

There is a reason the Father wants you to tithe. It's not just so there will be meat in his house (Malachi 3:10). It's so He can open the windows of heaven and pour you out a blessing that there shall not be room enough to receive it.
Romans 8:16,17 The spirit itself beareth witness with our spirit, that we are the children of God: And if children, then heirs; heirs of God, and joint- heirs with Christ; If so be that we suffer with Him, that we may be also glorified together.
Question.... How great is your source?

Revelation must be this: My source is God, most high possessor and maker of heaven and earth the deliverer of mine enemies.

In the beginning God said that as long as the Earth remains there will be seedtime and harvest Gen 8:22.
Saint Paul referred to the eternal law of sowing and reaping in Gal 6:7 "Be not deceived; God is not mocked; for whatsoever a man soweth, that he also reap".

Jesus constantly illustrated faith as a seed being planted to get results, comparing faith as a grain of mustard seed able to move mountains (troubles). Matt 17:20

Revelation is this. .If you have faith as a seed, if your believing becomes SEED-FAITH, even small as a grain of mustard seed, it will meet needs and problems that appear impossible, and as large as mountains before you. That is because each act of faith is a seed planted and will be multiplied many times.

Webster's defines Seed: The germ or source of something.
Webster's defines Plant: To put in the ground for growth.
Webster's defines Harvest: The result of any act, or process, to gather or reap.
Webster's defines Reap: To cut as with a sickle, or to gather or take, to get as a return, recompense, or result.

Example: A man was driving thru the area where delicious apples are raised, he saw refrigerated railcars and trucks being loaded to carry them to markets throughout America. Everywhere he looked nature was in production. Seed had been planted, the soil cultivated, and now the mighty reproduction forces had produced the harvest. God says in his word what ever you can conceive, and believe, you can do.

Webster's defines Conceive: To form, to imagine, to become pregnant with.

Example in Gen 11:6: The Lord said "The people are all in accord and nothing they have imagined they can do will be impossible to them".

In Deuteronomy 8:18: But you shall (earnestly) remember the Lord your God.
WHY? For it is He who gives you power to get wealth.
REASON: That He may establish His covenant which He swore to your fathers, as at this day.

GOD did what I'm telling you that you can do. God did it first and had it written as a blueprint for you to imitate HIS WORD. The Bible the manufactures hand book. The bible is the book of life. He already proved the concept, you don't have to try and re-invent the wheel, this works.

God conceived the world and man, He believed, and had faith. God believed in man enough to create him in His image with the power to choose good or evil, to live positively or negatively to believe or to doubt, to respond to God or denounce Him.

God believed so much in man even when he had gone his own way and sinned, that He sent His only begotten Son to earth to become a man and bring man to the place where he could be redeemed, given a new life and live abundantly.

Jesus, the seed God planted; through him God conceived every person becoming a new person, and imitating him, walking like him, talking like him, speaking his word. God has made it possible for each of us to conceive, to believe, and to get the right results. As we look around us, we see God blessing man. The harvest in the fields bursting forth from the tiny seeds planted months before and carefully tended; the farmer in control of the seeds he planted. The ground he sowed it in was designed to reproduce whatever was sown in it, and the inevitable was a harvest. God wants us to be blessed-to live abundantly.

You can face a need with your faith rather than doubt. Instead of becoming part of the problem you can become part of the solution. See a need exists to be met rather than existing to harass and intimidate you.
Problems are real, they exist, you don't have to pretend they don't exist. But you have the manufactures hand book to draw from.

Like 6:38 "Give and it shall be given unto you; good measure, pressed down, and shaken together, and running over, shall men give into your bosom. For with the same measure that ye mete withal it shall be measured to you again.

Philippians 4:19: My God shall supply all your need according to his riches by Christ Jesus.
Key1. God must be your whole source and you must believe it.

I will make a statement: Don't limit God. God is limitless. It is we who put God in a box.

I will tell you a story I read.
A farmer raised apples, peaches, apricots, cherries, pears, grapes, berries and several other fruit. His pride and joy was the big luscious Alberta peach.
People came from miles around to buy this peach. Years later, shocked to hear that it was all gone, so he was called and asked what happened?

Was it a storm?

Was there an invasion of insects? He said no it was not a storm nor was it an invasion of insects. It was Me.! Sadly he replied, I'll tell you what I did. As long as the fruit came each fall, I was satisfied to leave the trees along. They bore fruit and I thought my supply was the fruit. The fruit fed my family. We sold thousands of bushels for money and used the money. The fruit became everything to me. It was my business. I depended upon it. Everything I did; I judged according to how it related to the fruit. Then one year the crop was not so good. The next year it was less. That was when I stopped thinking about fruit and started looking to the trees. Before, I had paid attention to the trees. I cut the weeds and did a little plowing down each row. Then I woke up and realized that the peaches and the other fruit were just what they were – fruit of the tree. The supply was the tree. If I took care of the tree, the fruit would grow. Through poor understanding and haphazard care of the trees, I have only a few poor trees left. There's not enough fruit to pick anymore." Remember I told you that a lack of knowledge or what you don't know will hurt you. (in chapter 1).

There was a excitement in his voice and he said "But I'm putting in a young orchard. I've gone to the agricultural experts and learned how to take care of the fruit tree. So, I'm starting over. This time I'll take care of my source."

I will make another statement: It is more productive to give than to receive...

Revelation: For what we receive is not multiplied, but only what we give

Giving is necessary because: Every time you breathe. You must breathe out (give) to breathe in (receive), so is your very life, stop either exhaling or inhaling and you cannot live.

The farmer who plants (gives) a crop and, must give it to the earth. He must sow seed; otherwise, he will harvest (receive) only weeds. The seed he gives to the earth will be multiplied back to him, far greater in return than the amount planted.

Prayer must have the added essential of giving first (Thanksgiving). "Be careful for nothing; but in everything by prayer and supplication with thanksgiving let your requests be made known unto God" Philippians 4:6. The seed of thanksgiving with your prayer requests is an affirmation of God's return to you. Only what you give can God multiply back (return) to you again

Money is the medium of exchange. It is your, blood, sweat and tears, that represents your labor, your skill and effort, your whole self. When you give it, it represents yourself. The Bible says you are not your own...ye are bought with a price, therefore, Glorify God in your body, and in your spirit, which are God's." (1 Corinthians 6:19,20).

Jesus is interested in the multiplication of your seed-faith, because it is the multiplication of your self. A tree bringeth (return) forth....good fruit

KEY 2: What you give is the seed you plant. You plant wheat and you will get wheat. Plant peaches and you will get peaches. God says each after its kind.

If you want God to supply your financial needs, you will give seed money for Him to reproduce (return) and multiply. If your need is not money but something else, let the seed you give represent it. Use it as your point of contact to release your faith for God to meet this need.

Jesus says when you give freely, joyously, with full measure, then your giving will be multiplied back to you in the same spirit-GOOD MEASUE, PRESSED DOWN, AND SHAKEN TOGETHER, AND RUNNING OVER Luke 6:38

Steps...

A. PLANT
B. CULTIVATE
C. HARVEST- that which you planted.
Seldom can you plant and the Harvest comes quickly. There is a growing time for every seed that we plant and that includes our seeds of faith.

I'm glad you asked what a seed of faith is because I'm going to tell you. A seed of faith is something of value that we contribute to other people's lives. Its money and time we give to God or prayer we pray for other people. And when we wrap our faith around it, it becomes a carrier of life, a carrier of miracles.

Revelation
God himself is the good soil, soil that you can't see but which is eternal and ever abundant and faithful in reproducing my seed sown into harvest for me to receive.
When your tithes and offerings have gone from your hand, they become invisible, you can't see them, yet God is growing them invisibly but absolutely.
When Jesus was put on the cross God said "That's my seed to save human beings"
4. "God is rebuking the devourer for my sake" when I tithe.

God is not talking about raining dollars out of heaven, or a new house, or car, etc.
He's pouring things into your mind, your imagination, for you to dream and to vision (see) that which will change your life. That's the eternal Law.

A seedtime inevitably comes to a harvest time. After we have planted our seeds of faith we wait upon the Lord, That's where the faith part of seed-faith comes in, because our faith enables us to wait expectantly during the growing time of our seeds.

When you work you are encouraged to put away for retirement, using vehicles that your place of employment has established. It used to be that a company would put money in your plan without you putting any in it. The government urges you to set up a retirement program also and they will even give you some tax break.

All of these programs are designed to help you utilize your money wisely for your future. The plans and purpose of these financial programs are designed so that when you reach retirement age, the end of your working years, you will have a nest egg to live on, because social security along will not be enough, thus this will allow you to retire in dignity not poverty.

Many people do not realize that Almighty God has a financial plan for his people, which begins now and carries through eternity. And once you begin to get your life into proper relationship with Father God through Jesus Christ, and come into the knowledge of how to walk in the word of faith and power you will freely be a giver into the Kingdom of God.

I believe television was invented by God for the world to proclaim the Gospel, but because of the Church and the Christian, religion, tradition and denominationalism, we have allowed the devil to come in and steal television and use it for devilish purposes instead of for the Gospel.

Today through satellite communications, a program can be broadcast throughout the world at the same time, in their own language, without you having to go there. So the gospel has to be presented in context that will reach everybody and get their attention, because God is interested in everybody. And today TV and the Internet is that media.

God is interested in saving all, even the pimps, dope pushers, prostitutes, the president of AT&T and etc. Do you really think that the President of AT&T who commands a salary of $900,000 plus a year will come to church, or Bill Gates, yet Jesus died for ALL and he needs them to know that, but they will watch television?

Question   Where is all the money going to come from?

Answer   It has to come from God. Haggai 2:8 (AMP) says this: The silver is Mine and the gold is Mine. So then it is released in to the hands of God's kids to be used for the expansion of the kingdom of God on this earth.

Question   How the heck are you going to do it when you don't have any money honey? You cannot pay your bills now. You are beating your head against the wall trying to figure out how to get ahead, economically in this world.

Revelation: You get an increase in your wages, then the costs of bacon goes up, the costs Bread goes up, the costs of gasoline goes up, then your rent goes up, then your electricity goes up.

Get the picture. The world's economic system is not designed for you to get ahead it is designed to keep your nose to the grindstone.

Here's some more revelation. Miss a day's work and it will probably throw you 6 months behind or let me say it this way, you won't be able to keep your nose above water.

Truth: It is all a systematic plan of Satan for you to keep your nose to the grindstone.

The sad part is that even most Christians are in the same boat as the unbeliever, they owe their soul to the company store. They want to tithe, and give. But they can't, because they owe everything they make and have to pay it out in monthly payments, and Lord help should something break, we have to rob Peter to pay Paul and then they are broke too.
 So we must break this cycle of poverty, or else it will continue to go around like a merry go round. You see the bible says you must work. Wind falls are not the answer, look at those who have won the lottery, and what happened to them.

Father God has a plan whereby you can become financially and materially independent of the circumstances. That plan is initiated through tithes and offerings. Once you learn how to operate in God's financial plan, you will reach a point where you will have it to give it away.

Truth: God's principle is this! GIVE. the more you give, the more you get. The World's principle is this: KEEP.. The more you get Keep.

Revelation: You cannot give what you don't have, and if Satan has his way you never will.

Key: Tithing and Giving is part of the package of Salvation.

Prosperity is the will of God. 3 John 2 (AMP) says this: Beloved, I pray that you may prosper in every way and (that your body) may keep well, even as (I know) your soul keeps well and prospers. In other words God wants us to prosper in all areas.

You cannot be a blessing until you are blessed

Since God made Abraham very rich yesterday, He can make us rich today.

Mal 3:6; says I am the Lord and I change not.

Hebrews 13:8; He is the same yesterday, today, and forever.
It is conditional, that you obey God, be obedient to the Word of God

Questions
Has God lost his ability to make a man great?
Has God lost his ability to prosper man materially?
Has God lost his ability to prosper man financially in this world?

God will bless you beyond your wildest dream expectations. But you have to do it his way.

Let me burst your bubble
Spirituality has nothing to do with what you have or do not have. It has to do with your heart relationship with God.
You can be very spiritual and have nothing physically or materially.
You can be very spiritual and have everything physically and materially.
Physical and material things are irrelevant to your spirituality, unless you allow these things to influence you and affect your spirituality.

In Psalms 1:1; the very first word is blessed. It covers everybody. God is no respecter of persons.

In Psalms 1:1-3: blessed is the man that walketh (1.) not in the counsel of the ungodly, (2.) nor standeth in the way of sinners, (3) nor sitteth in the seat of the scornful, But his delight is in the law (or the word) of the Lord; and in his law (or Word) doth he mediate day and night. And he shall be like a tree planted by the rivers of water, that bringeth forth his fruit in his season; his leaf also shall not weather; and whatsoever he doeth (means to include financial security, means you can invest money wisely and profit from it. It does not say fail but shall prosper. It means that your relationship husband and wife should prosper; it means that parents should prosper in raising their kids. It says walk not in the counsel of the ungodly and you shall prosper.

If you obey and meet the conditions you shall prosper.

3 John 2 says. Beloved, I wish above all things that thou mayest prosper and be in health, even as thy soul prospereth.

Whether or not you succeed whether or not you are prosperous materially or financially, is not based on God. It is not up to God. IT IS UP TO YOU! You see God already did it all once and said he gave us the dominion in this earth.

You might be saying "Well God I am waiting on you, I am waiting on you to bless me, I am waiting on you to make it work, I am waiting on you to do your will. But God is saying I am waiting on you child. YOU DO SOMETHING. I am waiting on you.

YOU HAVE NO RIGHT TO ANYTHING YOU HAVE NOT PURSUED PEOPLE SEE WHAT YOU ARE BEFORE THEY HEAR WHAT YOU ARE WHATEVER YOU CAN TOLERATE YOU CANNOT CHANGE.

CHAPTER 4

Tithe Is The First Tenth

Leviticus 27:30: And all the tithe of the land, whether of the seed of the land or of the fruit of the tree, is the Lord's; it is holy to the Lord.

The foundational principle…..THINGS…The first things
1. CHILDREN
2. ANIMALS
3. CROPS
4. FRUIT OF THE TREE
5. WHATEVER-were to be to GOD. (God said, "I want the first portion of everything")

When Israel was a nation of farmers and shepherds, everyone owned land and livestock. Therefore, the first thing was easy because it was the firstborn or first fruits. God knew that the livestock and crops economy would gradually evolve to a monetary system. Thus God had to make a way for the giving of first things in a cash economy.

So if it is money, how much should it be? Well if it is redemptive work, do you know what God would say? "Let it be the tenth part".

The tithe means a tenth why a tenth?
TEN IN SCRIPTURE is always the number for redemption.
The tithes represent the whole of what was due from man to God, as marking and recognizing God's claim on the whole.

A. The first, God's sovereignty
B. Ten Camels-for Isaac's wife, Rebecca.
C. Ten donkeys-sent to bring Israel to Egypt.
D. Ten Plagues-used to free the Israelites from Egypt
E. Ten Commandments-for the Israelites to obey.

F. The tenth completes the eternal cycles
G. Antichrist's world power is comprised in the ten kingdoms, symbolized by the ten toes on the feet of the image of Nebuchadnezzar's dream and the ten horns of the fourth beast of Daniel's dream. (Dan 2:41; 7:7,20,24; Rev 12:3; 13:1, 17:3,7,12)

Anytime there is a redemptive work in progress, there will be a number ten involved. Ten plagues and then the children of Israel were redeemed out of Egypt. There were Ten Commandments, and God said, "If you will obey these ten things, I will redeem you".

I hope you understand that God could have thought of more than ten things to require of His people. But every time ten is used, God is working to buy back that which HE desires.

Here is the question?
If the tenth is a type of redemption, then why must it be first?

Answer. Because when it's given first it breaks the curse of destruction off the remaining 90%, releasing it to be used for its purpose.

In an effort to get at God and to try to hurt him, satanic forces are attacking the home, which is the closest thing on earth to God's heart. Homes are hurting and many times we do not understand why. This attack is more than just an attack on the home; for every time you find a new chapter about to be opened in God's great work you will find increased satanic activity. The enemies of God are following a practice that began a long time ago.

When Moses was born and the plan of God began to unfold so that the children of Israel would be brought out of the land of Egypt, God prepared a small child whose mother recognized that he was very special and Satan made an effort to fight against God's plan. Satan didn't know whom God had chosen, so he put it into the heart of the king (Pharaoh) to kill every child below a certain age so that he could get rid of the one baby who was going to have a definite part in the unfolding of God's plan.

Another time was when a decree was given in Shushan. The enemy knew that the time was almost here for the great deliverance of Israel, so he worked through the heart of a man named Haman. A decree went out that all of the Jews were to be slain. Again the enemy tried to stop God's plan, but he did not succeed.

When Jesus was born, the greatest chapter of all times began to unfold. Again the satanic forces said, "We have to stop him. He is God's own Son. We have to stop this deliverer, but we don't know where he is." They inquired, "Where is he? Where is he going to be born?"

If Satan could have read minds all he would have had to do was to go to the shepherds or the wise men and read their minds, but they weren't telling! King (Herod) discovered the general area, so that same satanic force went into operation. Once again all the babies were killed. But Jesus wasn't there!

And today, what's unfolding is God is bringing into focus the families of the earth. He is letting them know that his plan of salvation, a principle he put into operation years and years ago, is not just a plan for a single person. He reserves a place for the whole family, but each member must individually be born again. God gave this plan to Moses in the tabernacle.

God wanted the name of every head of the house and his family included in the gate of the tabernacle; the silver sockets, which held the veil of the temple, were to be made out of the shekels of their redemption. These sacrifices of half a shekel of silver were made by each man as a ransom for his soul unto the Lord. The shekels were to be melted, and the gates were to hang on the very fact that God has included ALL in his plan.

This redemption plan for the families was so important to God that he required each family to give a memorial offering of half a shekel every year so they wouldn't forget. (Exo30:12-16 38:25-28)

The enemy wants to spoil God's plan by hurling heavy artillery into the homes, causing husbands to lose feelings for their wives; causing restlessness; causing things to fall apart; causing children and parents to hate each other.

But God says Satan is not going to get away with it! God has decreed in His word that He will not fail and that an irreversible force is set in motion that nothing can stop. It has to happen! The only part of the equation is us.. We can choose to stand on God's word and believe or not too.

You see God has predestined the event, but not the individuals. He said, "If you will link arms with me, there will be joy and happiness in it for you.

I have FORE-ORDAINED you to be a partner with me in the great work that I am doing, but I will not hold you to it."

God is at work! The enemy is at work! These are the two opposing forces; But God has already decreed that he is the winner

Pray this prayer out loud

Father in the name of Jesus and by the authority of your word I call forth the riches that have been heaped together for the last days to come to us. The wages that have been withheld by fraud, and not receiving our harvest that the prophets have spoken over us, or the hundred-fold return from our sowing. We receive it now in Jesus name and cover it with the blood of Jesus.

I bind the beggarly spirit and loose the spirit of abundance. I bind the spirit of financial limitation and loose the spirit of multiplication. We are anointed to receive money.

I call for the wealth of the sinner that has been released to find its way to us to come into our hands now. Money you have been laid up, but we call it into manifestation now.

I call forth your power to get the covenant wealth that was promised to our forefathers to come into manifestation now for the end-time harvest of souls.

I call forth the wealth and riches to come into our house; and our righteousness to endure for ever according to the word.

We say devil, you get out of our business. We are reclaiming all the enemy territory that you tried to steal, and since you the devourer are a seed eater, you can't have our land.. You did not sow on our land so you can not reap our harvest. God said he would rebuke the devourer on our behalf. Stop it that's enough. We command you to leave and we call for the restoration seven times what was stolen from us in the name of Jesus. Amen

CHAPTER 5

Tithing Or Tipping

Now here is where we kick over sacred cows… Do you know it is possible to be giving 10% of your income and not be tithing?

If the tithe is not first, it is only an offering. God will bless offerings, but the redemptive blessing is reserved for the first portion. And so the blessing of the tithe is not on that which remains.

Lay out ten coins.
Ask these questions in the light of the truth just shared?
If these coins represent my income for the week, how many coins do I owe God for the week (ONE) correct. Every Christian in the world knows that but here comes the revelation in this question.
Which coin represents my tithe?   The first one! The first one is the only one that carries the power of redemption.   All of the remaining coins are" redeemed" because of what is done with the first one.
How do we know which coin is the first one? It's the first one spent…

Tithe is given first in faith to guarantee God that HE deserves first place because of who he is, not what HE provides.

It can be 10%, but if it is not the first fruits it doesn't count as tithe, it is just an offering. An offering is good and is usually inspired by a blessing or the word of God. And offerings help the work of ministry, but they don't establish Lordship.

Ever one has heard this story,

Gen 4:2-7
Now Able kept flocks, and Cain worked the soil. And in the course of time Cain brought to the Lord an offering of some of

the fruit of the ground. And Abel brought of the FIRST BORN of his flock and of the fat portions. And the Lord had respect and regard for Abel and his offering, but for Cain and his offering, HE had no respect or regard. So, Cain was exceedingly angry and indignant, and looked sad and depressed. And the Lord said to Cain, 'Why are you so angry? And why do you look sad, and depressed and dejected? If you do what is right, will you not be accepted? But if you do not do what is right, sin is crouching at your door: it desires to have you, but you must master it.

NOW let's lift the cover for a moment

Ten means redemption. And God says the first tenth is holy. In the Old Testament people had cattle, grain, food, children, and etc. He asked for the first tenth to come to him, because it is holy.

The story is really about their method of giving.
Abel brought an offering of the firstborn,
Cain brought only an offering of some of his increase
God blessed Abel and warned Cain
Cain was clearly disobeying   for God said, "If you do what is right, will you not be accepted?"

The difference between the two
Abel's offering was the first portion
Cain's was not
Abel put God first
Cain did not
Cain did not make him Lord, and therefore he was vulnerable to sin.

The order of that which is given to Him clearly defines His place in your life.
God does not need what we are giving!
HE IS GOD!
HE owns the cattle of a thousand hills

He had it before you earned it, and He'll have it after you're done with it.
What HE does need is the First, because that is the portion reserved for Him.
When the first is given, it buys back (or redeems) all that remains from the curse of destruction

Law of First
Things are created for our benefit. However, if we disobey and keep what belongs to Him, the first things become a curse to us. God called "the devoted thing" accursed if we withhold it? God said, "If you don't redeem your firstborn donkey, then break its neck. If you ride my donkey, unredeemed, it will become a curse to you. God never intended for us to bring the curse upon ourselves.

Success or failure?
When we put the Lord first, He stops the power of the destroyer in our lives. More importantly, we prove not only to God His importance in our lives, but we reinforce that in our own minds.

When you take the first tenth and use it for food, bills, etc. It opens the door to all vices, sins, diseases, and troubles that was in Pandora's Box. But when you give the first tenth, God said he will open the windows of heaven and pour you out a blessing that there will not be room enough to receive and he will rebuke the devourer over your finances.

God says the things that were in Pandora's Box are still there in the church. Webster's dictionary defines Pandora's Box (In Greek Mythology) she was the first woman: and was told not to open Pandora's Box, but her curiosity got the best of her and she opened the box.

Instantly all the evils that might plague humankind flew out except one which was left; and she closed the box.

These four things came out instantly:

1. Vices—Immoral habits or traits; habitual indulgence in degrading or harmful practices, Corruption, Iniquity, Immorality, Crime, Guilt, Prostitution, Lewdness, Lust, Sodomy, Fornication, Adultery, Incest.

2. Sins—a transgression of a law having divine authority. Lying, Cheating, Gossiping, Slander, Unforgiveness, Hatred, All ungodliness, Disobedience.

3. Disease—a condition of ill health or malfunction in a living organism; any disorder or unwholesome condition. Malady, Infirmity, Illness, Cancer, Diabetes, Heart trouble, High Blood Pressure, Stress 50-80% of illnesses are from stress. How do we react and chemicals.

4. Troubles—the state of being distressed, annoyed, upset, afflicted, or confused. Distress, Worry, Agitate, Vex, Anxiety, Depression.

We go back to the word now and see what it tells us about the vices, sins, diseases, and troubles in Pandora's Box, and what we find Isaiah told the whole story in three verses.

Isaiah53:4-6:(AMP)Surely He hath borne our grief's, (sicknesses, weaknesses, and distresses and carried our sorrows and pains (of punishment) yet we (ignorantly) considered Him stricken, smitten, and afflicted by God (as if with leprosy). But He was wounded for our transgressions, He was bruised for our guilt and iniquities: the chastisement (needful to obtain) peace was upon Him, and with the stripes (that wounded) Him we are healed and made whole. All we like sheep have gone astray; we have turned everyone to his own way: and the Lord has laid on Him the guilt and iniquity of us all.

Only the fifth one stayed in.

5. Hope—to desire with expectation of fulfillment. Hebrews 11:1 Faith is the substance of things hoped for. All the promises of God are yea and amen. Healing, Prosperity, Forgiveness, Blessings

Why then have the gates of hell prevailed against the church? People run here and there to be prayed for, to be prophesied over, to get help, but are still hurting on the inside.

Isaiah 1:4-6 (AMP) tells us why. Ah, sinful nation, a people loaded with iniquity, offspring of evil doers, sons who deal corruptly! They have forsaken the Lord, they have despised and shown contempt and provoked the Holy One of Israel to anger, they have become utterly estranged (alienated). Why should you be stricken and punished any more (since it brings no correction)? You will revolt more and more. The whole head is sick, and the whole heart is faint (feeble, sick and nauseated). From the sole of the foot even to the head there is no soundness or health in (the nation's body)—but wounds, and bruises and fresh and bleeding stripes; they have not been pressed out and closed up or bound up or softened with oil.

Let's take a quick peek at what the Bible says:

The children of Israel received divine protection, favor, healing, and provision because of the seed they sowed. If the seed you sow is good and it's planted in good ground, it will produce. But you also have to sow your seed with the right motives.

You don't give just to get something from God.
You can't buy the blessings and anointing of God.

Acts 8 tells why:
Simon the magician tries to do this very thing. When he tried to buy the blessings of God, the apostle Peter tells him:

"Your money perish with you, because you've thought that the blessings of God, may be purchased with money (Acts 8;20).

Giving must always be done from a right heart and a right spirit. And you must give with the right motives, and your seed must be good seed.

A. It has to be the first fruits
B. God wants your best, not you're left over.
C. God doesn't want a polluted offering (foul or unclean)

A son honoureth his father. A servant his master, so if God be your Father, where is his honor. Don't offer polluted bread upon his altar.

Malachi 1: 6-10: is talking about those who are in the ministry, that they must give properly before sharing on tithing and giving.

We must give God our best. Best implies top, purest, finest superior.
Instead of giving their best lamb as an offering on the altar to God in Malachi 1, they gave him one that was diseased
(thinking God wouldn't notice). And instead of giving God the finest showbread, they gave Him polluted bread…God knows what is your best and what is superior and what your flesh is comfortable giving.

Questions

Why do we have to give these offerings?
Why do we have to give so much in the offering?
Why can't God be satisfied with this?
How come He has to ask for the very best lamb I've got?
How come the best bread I've got?
How come the best everything I have?
Doesn't he know that hurts me?
I can't afford that?

This is what they were saying. "And God replied you have contempt for MY table" Nothing has changed.
Today we are still saying, "I'm not giving my money to those preachers". They are just lining their pockets! Look at all the things they have!

First off God is going to hold you responsible for whether you did what He said in His word you should do. God will not accept excuses

What we don't recognize is the quality of the seed we give, is the quality of our return, and were not talking about the amounts.

Jesus said in Mark 12 about the woman who gave two "mites" in the collection plate. The rich men put large sums of money in the offering. Yet Jesus said that she gave more than they did. You see Jesus is talking about the quality of her seed she gave the best that she could give.

Sometimes God may require of us more than we think we can give. He thinks our best is more than we think it is. And that is because God knows what our best is truly. He wants to get you out of the natural and over into faith. Giving what is comfortable to your flesh is not your best. There is no faith in that. Faith is when you get over into deep water.

Let me ask you this?   Do you believe Curses are real? I know you tell me you don't believe in that stuff.

Proverbs 3:33: (AMP) The curse of the Lord is in and on the house of the wicked, but He declares blessed (joyful and favored with blessings) the home of the just and consistently righteous. American Heritage defines a curse as "evil or misfortune to befall a person or thing, to invoke evil upon. Curses give demons the legal right to carry out their wicked plans.

I'm going to ask you some questions.

Does failure and frustration seem to be your lot in life?
Is your life full of continual setbacks and misfortunes?
Does it seem that no matter what you do in life, you cannot obtain the blessings of the Lord?
Are there serious marital problems?
Are there chronic financial problems?
What are you speaking?

Statement
The worse part is that you are a born again spirit filled believer and love the Lord.

Revelation   Well Good news is that you have been redeemed from the Curse, according to Gal. 3:13. Christ purchased our freedom.

We need to know the difference between what is ours legally and what is ours because we know. By that I mean …Someone can give you something and you take possession of it. Or someone can tell you that it is yours and you take possession of it by knowledge.

Now here comes more Revelation
Because something is legally yours, it does not mean you will automatically obtain it and walk in it. Our adversary, the devil, is determined to keep away from us what is legally ours. If he can keep you ignorant of what is legally yours, he can still enforce a curse against you, even though legally you are redeemed from it.

Sickness and disease…The word teaches that we are already healed by the stripes of Jesus. But we have to appropriate this promise by faith, which was sent 2000 years ago when Christ died on the cross.

Statement: Healing is a part of our redemption, but it is not automatic. We must appropriate it by faith. Or in other words receive it by faith. The believer may have to fight the good fight of faith for healing. The promises in the Word of God are not automatic, they are conditional.

Let me pull the covers off so to speak and unveil a truth.
Financial Perversion, why Terry whatever are you talking about. Financial Perversion includes the misuse of money.
Unjust gain and I know nobody in church is a cheat or liar because you are in church.
Also includes illegal trafficking of drugs, alcohol, robbery and embezzlement.
Here's the kicker not honoring God (BY TITHING).

Here is the Revelation.
These sins or a history of these sins in the bloodline can open the door for the Curses of Poverty.

Come on Terry what are you telling me?
A. The result of all sin is death and destruction
B. Destruction is the action or process of destroying something. Curses open the door for the spirit of destruction to work with other spirits to destroy certain areas of an individual's life.
C. Destruction of the Mind….Mental Illness, Insanity, Madness and Confusion
D. Destruction of the Finances…Includes spirit of poverty, lack, debt and financial failure
E. Destruction of the Body, are spirits of sickness, infirmity, disease and plagues
F. Destruction of the Family, are spirit of death, accidents, rebellion, alcohol, strife.

Curses come as a result of God's divine justice, recompensing the iniquity (perversion) of the fathers into the bosom of the children in the form of curses, causing sorrow of heart and opening the door for evil spirits, giving them legal right to persecute and destroy by carrying out their evil devices in the lives of people under curses.

Be careful what you say.

Have you ever said, I take one step forward and two steps backward

Nothing ever seems to work out for me

I never can seem to get ahead

I knew something bad would happen

If it were not for bad luck, I wouldn't have any luck at all

This always happens to me

It happened to my parents and now its happening to me

What you are saying indicates where some of the issues are, and since this is about tithing that is all we will expose.

Financial Problems: History of debt, bankruptcy, poverty and lack in the family.

Financial Setbacks mean to hinder to delay.

Haggai 1:6 Ye have sown much, and bring in little, ye eat, but ye have not enough; ye drink, but ye are not filled with drink; ye clothe you, but there is none warm; and he that earneth wages earneth wages to put it into a bag with holes.

Let's say it this way. Your income disappears, as though you were putting it into pockets filled with holes.

Look at what is happening..

Not able to get ahead financially

Unable to keep jobs, layoffs

Inability to find work, with no logically explanation

Never seem to escape unexpected bills

Accidents causing additional bills

Loss of money

Car breakdowns,

Mechanical malfunctions

Losing money (purse or wallet)

Loss to thief

High interest rates

Just when you seem to get ahead financially something happens to set you back even if you earn a lot of money

Proverbs 10:15 (AMP) The rich man's wealth is his strong city: the poverty of the poor is their ruin
Ps 52:7 (AMP) See, this is the man who made not God his strength-(his stronghold and high tower); but trusted and confidently relied on the abundance of his riches, seeking refuge and security for himself through his wickedness.

I Tim 6:17 (AMP) As for the rich in this world, charge them not to be proud and arrogant and contemptuous of others, nor to set their hopes on uncertain riches but on God, Who richly and carelessly provides us with everything for (our) enjoyment.

You remember when I said you have to break the cycle. Webster says…A cycle is "an interval of time during which a sequence of a recurring succession of events or phenomena is completed; a course or series of events or operations that recur regularly and usually lead back to a starting point."

Something has to change
Something has to move
The cycle has to be broken, and the abundance cycle must be started.
The thing that has to move is that old thinking process that continues to bring you to the insufficiency you have lived with for so long. Now let Jesus make all things new

Now in Haggai 1:7 The prophet says this "Consider your ways"
The people were in this condition because of their ways.

In order to come out from under the curse, we must change our ways. Often people living under a curse never take time to consider their ways.

TO CONSIDER: means to think of especially with regard to taking some action. It means to reflect or deliberate.

Then you need to repent which means to turn from your wicked ways, without repentance there is no deliverance. When you repent, you turn around and turn away from sin

Now you can bring your tithe your tenth of your income into the storehouse where you are fed the word so there might be meat in mine house and prove me now by it says the Lord of host, if I will not open the windows of heaven for you and pour you out a blessing, that there shall not be room enough to receive it.

Things to remember:
1…Don't forget God.   Remember God.
2…God is your Source of supply
3…God's promise (covenant) is that you will be blessed, so that you can bless others.

Remember the Lord your God, for He is your source of supply who gives you the ability and power to get wealth   Deut 8:18

Without his help you cannot be wealthy. Even if you gain all the world's riches, but fail to give God first place in your life, you will not enjoy them .Ecclesiastes 6:2

God told Abraham that he would have a child and the child would be his seed and that through him all nations of the earth would be blessed.

Then God told Abraham how it would happen. He said, "I AM El Shaddai."

Let me paraphrase it this way:
I'm going to give you a child by the sum total of Who I Am and what I can do.
My Name is El Shaddai.
I Am the Almighty; I have the power to carry out my will.
I Am the God who can cause results in your life.

"I AM" means the Uncaused One who can cause or create all things.

In Hebrew, "El" means might or power and is often used in a violent sense; while "Shaddai" describes a different power, that of all bountifulness.

The word itself means breasted. This gives "El Shaddai" the complete meaning of the Power or Shedder forth of blessings, temporal and spiritual.

Hence, as by her breast, the mother has almost infinite power over the child, so God reveals His power over us through His bountifulness. His Almightiness, like that of the breast, is a bountiful, self-sacrificing love, giving and pouring itself out for you. He quiets your restlessness. He nourishes and strengthens you. He draws you back unto Himself when you are in danger.

God told Abraham that he was the all breasted one, the nourisher, strengthener. God said "I AM whatever you need Me to be in your time of need. I AM a God who is full of life, vitality, and creativity. If you will nurse and draw strength from Me, you'll bring forth fruit." When He becomes EL Shaddai to you, then He is whatever you need Him to be.

Paul had a revelation of EL Shaddai, the Almighty God: But my God shall supply ALL of your need according to his riches in glory by Christ Jesus Philippians 4:19   Paul's revelation of this truth in Philippians 4:19 is "Relative to the living conditions of Heaven and in agreement with the truth and the will of God"
Jesus instructs us to pray this way. Matthew 6:10-11….."Lord, Thy will be done in earth…give us this day our daily bread (strength and inspiration for our livelihood)"
So when you become a Christian, you don't have to think you will never have anything again.

Statement: God is not opposed to your having things!

Revelation of that Statement: He is opposed to those things having you. Matt 6:33... But seek ye first the kingdom of God, and his righteousness; and all these things shall be added unto you. God wants you to live in health and abundance in this life. God wants you to have the unspeakable joy of the Lord in this life. I'm not saying you won't have problems, I'm telling you that when you walk through the fire, the fire will not burn you, because God will walk with you through the fire! Isaiah 43:2...

Revelation1. When thou passest through the waters, I will be with thee;
Revelation2. And through the rivers, they shall not overflow thee;
Revelation3. When thou walkest through the fire, thou shalt not be burned; neither shall the flame kindle upon thee.

When you go through deep waters, you will not drown! God gives us the power over our problems and, in many cases, the power to remove them....

KEY 1 Mark 11:23: Whoever says to this mountain (trouble), Be lifted up and thrown into the sea! And does not doubt (lack of the word) at all in his heart, but believes (this is the faith action) that what he says will take place, it will be done for him.

Jesus gives us the keys to release, on earth, the will of God as it is in Heaven. Heaven is waiting for you to get your mind renewed to "the will of God (God's word) as it is in heaven," so you, can establish, demonstrate, and explain it by examples which come from your life. You are to be a living epistle which constantly demonstrates, reveals, shows, and mirrors the will of God as it is in Heaven.

Ephesians 5:1…Therefore be imitators of God-copy Him and follow His example-as well-beloved children (imitate their father) or say it this way…Walk like Him, Talk like Him, Act like Him, speak His Word.

Revelation Knowledge….
Rom 8:32. Freely give us all things
Ps 34:10. But they that seek the Lord shall not want any good thing
Ps 84:11. No good thing will He withhold from them that walk uprightly.
Ps 37:4.   And He shall give thee the desires of thine heart
Isa 1:19   If ye be willing and obedient, Ye shall eat the good of the land

Key 2. Mark 11:24: Therefore I say unto you, what things so-ever ye desire, when ye pray, believe that ye receive them, AND YE SHALL HAVE THEM.
3 John 2 Beloved, I wish (pray) above all things that thou mayest prosper and be health even as thy soul prospereth. Paraphrased I pray above all else that thou mayesth prosper physically, mentality, financially, sociality, and spirituality.

God gives us the power to get wealth and in Hebrew; that means to:
Get
Make
Create
Design
Invent
Bring forth
Procure
Bring into being
Cause to happen

God gives seed (ideas) to the sower; because when an idea is sown, it can reap a harvest. Isa 55:10. For as the rain cometh down, and the snow from heaven, and returneth not thither, but watereth the earth, and maketh it bring forth and bud, that it may give seed to the sower, and bread to the eater.

God delights in the prosperity of His servants. He said He is going to give us the wealth of the sinner. The sinner is the person who doesn't know how to operate in the spiritual laws. Success is not going to work for him anymore like it has been working, for God is judging the earth; and unless he is operating in spiritual laws, he is going to lose his wealth.

More Revelation:
Those of us who are operating in spiritual laws and who have learned to walk by faith, instead of in fear, are going to take the wealth out of his hands. The sinners are going to give the wealth to us just like the Egyptians gave their wealth to the children of Israel.

This Revelation will pop your bubble
Wealth is not just money. Money, actually, is the appearance of wealth. True wealth is not material possessions. True wealth is what you know and the level of your wisdom. The word wisdom or wise means in its simplest form, the ability to see.

Let me tell you a little story that illustrates this:
Henry Ford when he was 40 years old was making $20.00 dollars a week. Then he got an idea of mass producing automobiles. By the time he was 60, he was the richest man in the world. Some one asked him one day, "Mr. Ford, what would happen if you lost all your possessions? He said, "Sir, my wealth is not in material possessions; my wealth is in the information I know and the information I know how to get my hands on. "If everything were taken away, and I had no more material possessions or wealth, I would have it all back in less than five years because of the information I have.

Wealth is what you have inside you. That is why we say faith is the substance of things hoped for (Hebrews 11:1).Wisdom, (information, the word Of God), and the ability to see things correctly with your spiritual eyes will produce abundance in your life.

Wisdom gives you the ability to discern motives and actions, causes and effects, and the law of seedtime and harvest. Wisdom shows you ways to get money. So please remember the Lord in all that you do and especially in your tithes and offerings.

Now let me bring you more information and it is this; "First"- that which comes before all else, in produce that grows out of a previously planted seed or the fruit of one's labor. First fruit is a term used to describe the first fruit of the first harvest. God commanded his people to present the first fruit to the Levitical priesthood that served as food (Deuteronomy 26:2). In Israel, it marked the end of the barley growing season and the beginning of the wheat season. In ancient Israel, first fruits are mentioned in what is Shavuot, the Festival of Weeks.

This information was came from a on line historical source: Jews from all over the land of Israel made the journey to Jerusalem on Shavuot to offer their first fruits of the new season. The pilgrimage was one of three that was required of all Jews who were able. Shavuot, with its wheat offering in the Temple, also marked the end of a harvest cycle, which began when the barley crop was offered on Pesach. Barley was used as animal feed, whereas wheat was generally saved for human consumption. The two offerings represent the movement from the slave existence of Egypt (the Pesach offering) to the elevated experience of human beings created in the Divine image who enter into a relationship with God (the revelation at Sinai on Shavuot).

As the Israelites observed this important feast day, it took on even more in depth symbolism in the time of the Messiah (New Covenant). This biblical holiday Pentecost which literally means to count 50. Acts 2:1-4(AMP) says: And When the day of Pentecost had fully come, they were all assembled together in one place.

2. When suddenly there came a sound from heaven like the rushing of a violent tempest blast, and it filled the whole house in which they were sitting.

3. And there appeared to them tongues resembling fire, which were separated and distributed and which settled on each one of them.

4. And they were all filled (diffused throughout their souls) with the Holy Spirit and began to speak in other (different, foreign) languages (tongues), as the Spirit kept giving them clear and loud expression (in each tongue in appropriate words).

CHAPTER 6

The Law Of Nature

In Genesis 1:11,12: And God said, (action, faith, spoken word) Let: (reaction). The first law says for every action, there is a reaction. In other words an object at rest will stay at rest, and an object in motion will tend to stay in motion. Motion or lack of motion cannot change without unbalanced force acting. If nothing is happening to you, and nothing does happen, you will never go any-where. If you're going in a specific direction, unless something happens to you, you will always go in that direction.

Let's give you 4 keys on how this law works, to unlock doors for you. You have seen the TV program "Lets Make A Deal" and what is behind door number?
Which door will you choose and will you choose to use all the keys and open all the doors.
Listen well and hear with both your ears and your heart.

Revelation: Why faith would have meant holding fast to your confession knowing that it was working. For you must believe everything you said you must believe that everything will come to pass and this is where you release your faith in every word you speak. It says those things which (He God) spoke you must also speak in faith.

Truth: You have to set things in motion, even in the spiritual realm

Key1. Your faith and God's Word plus time Change Things

Key2. Saying and believing brings results when done in faith

Key3. You must develop faith in your words so you can believe what you are saying day after day will come to pass.

Key4. Set a watch over your mouth
So let us resume our subject on tithing.

Tithing must become a way of life, just like confessing God's word. When you first start, you don't see any changes but you keep doing it.

Believing God is a decision you must make. You don't always want to believe God. But you must make a decision to believe God. You don't wake up one morning and say I just feel like believing God today. You study and pray and get God's word in you so that no matter what it looks like in the natural even in the face of apparent defeat, even in the face of lack, even when things are going wrong you just believe God.

Ephesians 4:29-30... Let no corrupt communication proceed out of your mouth, but that which is good to the use of edifying, that it may minister grace unto the hearers. And grieve not the Holy Spirit of God. If you can't speak in agreement with God's word, then don't speak at all. There are some times we must force our mouth to speak and declare God's word over our situation and one of those situations is in our finances when we give our tithe. Luke 6:38.. Give, and (gifts) will be given you, good measure, pressed down, shaken together and running over will they pour into (the pouch formed by) the bosom (of your robe and used as a bag). For with the measure you deal out- that is, with the measure you use when you confer benefits on others-it will be measured back to you.

REVELATION Faith will come more quickly if you quote the word yourself.

KEY1. Your faith will never rise any higher than your confession. Your confession is the ceiling for your faith.

TRUTH: Without God's Word in you, there will be no faith. You have to take the Word of God and build it into your spirit, until you know, that you know, that you know God's Word is true in you, and when you are that sure, you will have a manifestation of it. The more highly developed you get in let's say fear, the quicker the manifestation will come or the more highly developed in faith, the quicker the manifestation will come.

TRUTH: Fear comes by hearing the words of the devil. Faith comes by hearing the God's Word

KEY2. Practice what you preach, set it in motion, get it working in your life. You must say what the word of God says.

I am a tither and I give offerings and therefore I receive your promise to me that you will pour out blessings to overflowing and that you personally will rebuke the devourer over everything I have, because as I pray and believe your word it shall not return unto you void, but it shall accomplish what you please and shall prosper in supplying everything I need.

You even said that if I reverence you and delight greatly in your commandments, I will receive wealth and riches in my house and the righteousness that endureth for ever. And I thank you Father that your promises are Yea and Amen, and when I give for Your sake and the Gospel's that I can expect to receive a hundred times as much as I gave now in this time as well as houses and lands and family.

Elijah heard the sound of the abundance which means…a noise, tumult (commotion, uproar) wealth, rumbling, riches and then he went to the mountain and prayed to God for the abundance of rain. You see he began to expect the manifestation of what he was praying for and even when his servant said he didn't see the evidence he kept sending him back until he saw the cloud like a man's hand. That was all Elijah needed because he knew his prayer had been answered and the rain would come. He began making preparations to leave the city before the rain and he outran the chariot that 30 miles.

Isaac sowed his seed in famine, when everyone else was hoarding their seed or fleeing to Egypt.

The widow at Zarephath fed the man of God first from the last bit of meal and the meal did not fail and cruse of oil did not run out until the rain came.
The poor widow at the temple gave all of her living as an offering.
The Word of God is our guide to financial blessings, but the seed must be sown on good ground.

2 Chronicles 20:20 (AMP) Believe in the Lord your God, so shall ye be established; believe his prophets, so shall ye prosper.
Jeremiah 30:3 (RVS) for behold, days are coming, says the Lord when I will restore the fortunes of My people Israel and Judah. Says the Lord, and I will also bring them back to the land that I gave to their fathers, and they shall take possession of it.

Let me start you out with some faith building.

The Kingdom inside of you is the kingdom of God. Jesus is in that kingdom.
Philippians 4:19: My God shall supply all your need according to his riches in glory (HOW?) by Jesus Christ.
Well who is Jesus Christ (THE WORD OF GOD) and He is going to do it by the Word of God.

Well how does the Word of God work? The word of God works in the human spirit the same way food taken in to the physical body works in the physical body. You eat food, natural food. It is assimilated in the body and produces a power called strength. When the Word of God is received into the human spirit, it does basically the same thing. It is assimilated in the human spirit and produces a force called faith; a spiritual force called faith which is spiritual power. That force comes from the Word of God. In the Heart...In the Mouth The word is nigh thee, even in thy mouth, and in thy heart: that is, the word of faith, which we preach ROM 10:6-8

The Cycle: See the word first gets in your mouth, then it gets in your heart, which corresponds with what Proverbs 3:3 says: write these things "upon the tablet of your heart." And David says in Ps 45:1."My tongue is the pen of a ready writer." And Jesus said in Matt 12:35."A good man out of the good treasure of his heart bringeth forth good things."

KEY1.The kingdom of God is as if a man cast seed into the ground.

The Apostle Paul says the Word has to:
1. get into your mouth first
2. then it gets in your heart.

Example: Tape your voice on a tape recorder and play it. Your voice is picked up by your inner ear and fed into your human spirit, the bible says (HEART),then you plant the seed of Gods word in your heart by speaking it.

Guess what happens when you speak the Word of God?
When you speak the Word out of your mouth, then you are planting a seed, And not only that, "Faith cometh by hearing, and hearing by the Word of God" RO 10:17

Revelation: The more you speak the Word, the more you believe it. The more you believe it, the Word, the more you speak it.
2 Corinthians 4:13: we having the same spirit of faith, according as it is written, I believed, and therefore have I spoken. I also believed and therefore speak.

So let's put this revelation in a cycle of truth:
What you believe, you will speak.

If you believe the Word, you will speak it.
If you speak it, you will believe it,
And if you believe it, you'll speak it
And if you speak it, you will believe it
This is God's cycle for producing faith as well as planting seed for harvest.

It's in your mouth, and it's in your heart. When it's in your heart in abundance, it gets in your mouth. Out of the abundance of the heart the mouth speaketh. What ever is in your heart it will always tell on you?

If you are in doubt and fear and unbelief, you will talk about it.
If you are in faith, you will talk about it.

Let me finish the truth about KEY1 and this is it.
Jesus said the Kingdom of God is as if a man cast seed into the ground. God is not sowing seed for you, and just because you read it in the Bible, it's not going to manifest unless you do it.
If you are a farmer and you say I'm going to leave my farming to God, and whatever grows out there will be God's will for me. What do you think you will get? I bet you don't get anything good to eat or sell.
That is because the earth is under a curse and you must force it to produce good things .You have to plant good seeds. Jesus says the kingdom of God is as if a man cast seed into the ground and he should sleep and rise night and day. The seed should spring up and grow, he knows not how, for the earth brings forth fruit of herself. Confessing God's Word is a process, It's a way of Life. It takes time to build faith.

This is the financial image we need to have. Any believer can conceive God's Word concerning finances by being obedient to the promise, give, and it shall be given unto you. When you give, then start confessing this: It is given unto me, good measure, pressed down, shaken together and running over, will men give unto my bosom. I have favor with God and men, and I sow bountifully. I reap bountifully. My God makes all grace abound toward me, and I, having all sufficiency of all things, do abound to all good works. Luke 6:38 II Corinthians 9:6,8

If you sow seed with the right motive, then you can be sure it will produce a harvest.

The question is? What kind of harvest will you reap?
In the natural realm, with the law of Nature in operation, which says everything produces after its own kind. If you cut open an apple, you will find apples seeds inside, not orange seeds or watermelon seeds. The Word says that everything produces after its own kind, and that seed is in itself. (Gen 1:11)

Now people produce people, and dogs produce dogs, so if scientists say other than that, they are wrong, donkeys produce donkeys, donkeys don't produce people. Sometimes people produce people who act like donkeys, but that is only because no one disciplined them when they were children. Horses don't produce tigers, and apples don't produce oranges. Everything produces after its own kind, which is the Law of Nature (Gen1:11,12). The fact that everything produces after its own kind is the natural flow of the earth.

Thank God: giving is not bound to just the natural laws of this earth. The law of Nature does not apply when you get over into the realm of the spirit.

Key: When you get over into exercising faith, which is a spiritual act, you supersede natural law. Jesus said my "My Words are spirit, and they are life" (John 6:63). When you act on God's word and what God said to do, you supersede natural law.

El Shaddai: "One who can supersede all natural laws. God can speed things up, and He can slow things down. He can do something totally different than the way it's always been done. The laws of nature don't bind El-Shaddai. (El is a shortened form of Elohim. It sets forth the might, the strength, and the excellence of God. Shad is the Hebrew word for breast. Shaddai picture's God's fullness or bounty his tenderness his generosity, his desire to nurture us and make us fruitful.

Hebrews 7:8 (AMP) Furthermore, here (in the Levitical priesthood) tithes are received by men who are subject to death, while there (in the case of Melchizedek), they are received by one of whom it is testified that he lives (perpetually).

We are still witnessing that Jesus is not dead, but alive. The verse says that when men receive tithes given on the earth, Jesus also receives them.

Revelation: So the tithe is not just a physical act; it's also a spiritual act.
It gets over into the realm of the spirit. It will supersede the natural law of Genesis, the law that says everything produces after its own kind.
So when you sow a seed, you won't necessarily get back the thing that you have sown.

Question: If you sow money, and don't need money, then what good would it do you to reap money?

The law of Nature does not apply to the realm of the spirit. Instead, the spiritual laws of tithing and giving supersede the natural laws of sowing and reaping. When you give a seed, you can reap whatever it is that you need at the time.

Statement: What I'm really saying is that a seed sown in faith will meet any need. (More about this in chapter 10)

Here is an example of spiritual laws superseding natural laws (2 Kings: 4).
When the Shunammite woman gave to Elisha, the prophet of God, her need was met. She was already a very rich woman. A lack of money was not her problem. She wanted to have a baby.

In the natural, it was impossible. Her husband was so old he was physically not able to reproduce. The natural laws of reproduction made having a baby impossible. So the Shunammite woman acted upon the Word of God, which was the job for EL-Shaddai.

Now less look under the covers so to speak:
(2 Kings:4,8(AMP). One day Elisha went on to Shunem, where a rich and influential woman lived who insisted on his eating a meal. Afterward whenever he passed by he stopped there for a meal.

This woman was very rich. Every time Elisha the prophet of God came to town, she fed him. Then finally she suggested to her husband that they add a room onto their house so Elisha could stay there while he was in Shunem. (Verse 10) Let us make a small chamber, which cost money. If you build on a room for someone, that's a monetary gift.

After Elisha received the woman's gift, he asked her what she wanted God to do for her in return. She told him that she was well taken care of and didn't need anything. Then the prophet told his servant to find out what the woman needed. The servant came and told Elisha that the woman was without child.
(2Kings 4:8-14)

The scripture says the husband was very old, and in those days, if a woman went childless, she considered herself to be cursed. So this Shunammite's need was not money; her need was a child. Her need was for the power of God to come on her husband to cause his youth to be renewed like the eagles.

Elisha told her, "About this season (or the same time next year), according to the time of life, thou shalt embrace a son Verse 16.

The power of God must have come on her husband, because one year later, she had a bouncing baby boy. Her seed opened the door for her need to be met.

This woman's monetary seed did not produce after its own kind; she did not receive money in return for financial seed. But because that seed was sown in faith, the seed supernaturally met her need. She gave finances and received a child.

Your seed, obedience and faith depend on you. It's a decision that you will have to make.

So as I said God (El-Shaddai) is not bound by natural laws. When you get over into exercising faith, which is a spiritual act, you supersede natural law. God can speed up or slow things down, He can do something totally different than the way it's always been done.

I would like to interject a story recorded in the New Testament about the super natural by passing natural laws.

Matthew 14:22-36 which you should read: It says Jesus commanded his disciples to get into the ship and go to the other side while he sent the crowd away. And then Jesus went up into a mountain, praying into the evening. By this time the ship was in the midst of the sea, being tossed back and forth by the waves.

Now get this, in the forth watch (3am-6am) of the night. Jesus went to the ship walking on water. The word says the disciples saw him (Jesus) walking on the sea and they got into fear. But Jesus spake to them saying it is I (Jesus) don't be afraid.

And Peter then says to Jesus, bid me to come to thee on water. The rest of the story says Peter got out of the ship, which is more than most of us would do and he began to walk on water toward Jesus, but when he saw the wind boisterous, he was afraid; let his faith leave him; when he got his eyes on the circumstances and off Jesus, and he began to sink in the water. Jesus saved him, he didn't drown.

Do a faith thing, get excited about God's promises
By faith we stand on the Word of God
By faith we are who God says we are
By faith we are able to do what we do
We are the called of God by faith
We are the anointed of God, by faith
By faith we are the son's of God
By faith we inherit every promise of God
By faith His glory is being revealed in our lives

We are feeding faith to this word on the blessing of commitment, because we know the just shall live by faith (Romans 1:17; Gal 3:11; Heb 10:38)

Faith cometh by hearing and hearing by the word (Romans 10:17)

You are Abraham's seed why should you have less cattle, silver, and gold than the world?

Never look at the ground and say everything is bad for me, "When God told Abraham, Lift up now thine eyes, and look (Gen 13:14)

Every promise in the Word of God can be yours, if you believe and apply that promise to your life by Faith. All the promises of God come to you by faith. Salvation by Faith (Salvation not only means being saved but having solutions to every problem) Healing by Faith Financial Blessings by Faith

Key 1 Whatever you can see by faith, you can have if you will believe and not doubt. (More about this in Chapter: 13).

Revelation   All you need is to have the faith like a grain of mustard seed.

Have you ever seen a mustard seed? Well the period at the end of this sentence is the size of a mustard seed, and that is how much faith God says you need. (Matt 17:20).

Key 2 Your faith is the seed of life.

Revelation: First you do the spiritual act (plant the seed), then it produces the natural supply, so just believe and have a little bit of faith, then you can have what you see. (Mark 11:22-24)

Key 3 Faith activates the promises of God in your life and releases God to work for you, but faith has to be fed the word of God to keep it strong.

The word says Abraham was justified not by what he could do, but by what he believed God would do when he acted in obedience.

Revelation: The first thing the seed of faith does is to put down some roots, preparing a foundation to hold the stalk that is coming.

The bigger the stalk, the more roots that seed must put down and the longer the waiting period it takes for the whole thing to develop and build. If you attempted some things that did not turn out the way you thought, don't get discouraged.

Key 4 If you did not lose your faith, the word is still growing in your life and will bring forth fruit.

The bible says that all the promises in Christ are yea and amen II Corinthians 1:20. This means that Jesus Christ is not one to say "yes" when He means "no", he always does exactly what He says. He carries out and fulfills all of God's promises, no matter how many of them there are.

Revelation   God is not talking about looking with your natural eyes; He's talking about looking with your spiritual eyes.

Unless you can see your desire spiritually, you cannot believe it. When you see something in the word of God with your spiritual eyes, then you can believe it.
I'm talking about seeing it in your spirit through eyes of Faith. (Example: you must see your self successful and if not you won't be)

When Abraham was beyond the normal age of productivity, He had a son (Isaac) because he believed God. Through the eyes of faith, he saw what God had told him.

While we look at the things which are seen, but at the things which are not seen: for the things which are seen are temporal; (Webster defines as pertaining to the present life, worldly) but the things which are not seen are eternal.
2 Corinthians 4:18

Key 5   Don't look at the circumstances, Look at the things which are not seen in the natural, but only in the spirit.

Key 6   Look at the promises in God's Word.

Revelation: God's word will direct you even when you cannot see anything with your natural eyes.

When you see God's promises, you overcome the visible with the invisible. After you see the promise, you must go out and claim your possessions. You must have corresponding, actions of faith, and this requires work.

Key 7 Laziness will never get you God's blessings or prosperity.

Malachi 3:10 (AMP) says to do something…. Bring all the tithes. How much is all?   It's the whole tenth of your income. Where do I bring it?   You are to bring it into the store house. You mean the grocery store? No I mean here to the Church, that there may be food in my house, do you mean the kind of food I eat when I am hungry? No I mean the word that your spirit needs so it won't starve.

Prove Me now by it, says the Lord of Hosts, if I will not open the windows, (a period of time available or highly favorable for doing something) of heaven for you and pour you out a blessing, (a gift bestowed by God. The invoking of God's favor upon a person).Favor means preferential treatment, a gift bestowed as a token of regard or love, that there shall not be room enough to receive.

God told Abraham, Arise, Walk through the land. (Kingdom of God and his promises) Gen 13:17.
He had to act on his faith to possess his inheritance. You will too. You will need to walk out your possessions and work out your inheritance, or you can sit and look around, and say "Oh yes, that's nice." You can stay in your house, doing nothing, Can you imagine if Abraham had stayed in his tent doing nothing, the great nation Israel never would have existed. God's promises are founded on willingness and obedience, not wishful thinking.

When God tells you to walk out the land of your inheritance, He means it. If you are willing and obedient, you can:
1...Possess the land
2...Prosper
3...Have God's blessings
4...Possess the gates of every one of your enemies

Story 1 One day a farmer was out in his backyard, and the Spirit of the Lord said to him, "I want you to drill an oil well right here. The farmer, who had been faithful to give to God, obeyed; and within a few days he hit oil. That oil well produces about 600 barrels per day. At the time he drilled the well, oil was priced at $41.00 dollars per barrel. His daily backyard income came to $24,600 dollars."

That farmer had no idea there would ever be an oil well within 100 miles of him. He simply was willingly and obedient to God. Consequently, he now has 10 wells which average 2,000 barrels per day. If you calculated today's price of $83.00 dollars per barrel that would equal $166,000.00 a day. That's not bad pay for obeying the Spirit of God. Now today May 2010, Morgan Stanley predicts $95.00 by year end

Ps 24;1 Says "The earth is the Lord's, That includes what is on top of and what is underneath the earth. The cattle on a thousand hills, all the silver and the gold, and even the oil are all the Lord's. And He has covenanted to give you as much of it as you desire, if you will follow and obey him.

Story 2 A small congregation in the foothills of the Great Smokies built a new sanctuary on a piece of land willed to them by a church member. Ten days before the new church was to open, the local building inspector informed the pastor that the parking lot was inadequate for the size of the building.

Until the church doubled the size of the parking lot, they would not be able to use the new sanctuary. Unfortunately, the church with its undersized lot had used every inch of their land except for the mountain against which it had been built. In order to build more parking spaces, they would have to move the mountain out of the back yard.

Undaunted, the pastor announced the next Sunday morning that he would meet that evening with all members who had mountain moving faith. They would hold a prayer session asking God to move the mountain from the back yard and to somehow provide enough money to have it paved and painted before the scheduled opening dedication service the following week. At the appointed time, 24 of the congregation's 300 members assembled for prayer. They prayed for nearly three hours. At ten o'clock the pastor said the final "Amen".

"We'll open next Sunday as scheduled." He assured everyone. "God has never let us down before, and I believe He will be faithful this time too."

The next morning as he was working in his study there came a loud knock at his door. When he called "come in", a rough looking construction foreman appeared, removing his hard hat as he entered. "Excuse me, Reverend. I'm from Acme Construction Company over in the next county. We're building a huge shopping mall. We need some fill dirt. Would you be willing to sell us a chunk of that mountain behind the church? We'll pay you for the dirt we remove and pave all the exposed area free of charge, if we can have it right away. We can't do anything else until we get the dirt in allow it to settle properly."

The little church was dedicated the next Sunday as originally planned and there were far more members with "mountain moving faith" on opening Sunday than there had been the previous week!

CHAPTER 7

Obedience In Giving

Key: We are to command.

You and I, are to seek the kingdom of God first, and His righteousness, and all the things we have need of, He will provide.

1. He will pour out blessings of prosperity upon us.

2. Food, clothing, shelter, finances, and all these things we need to live on earth, shall be provided.

3. So the first thing is we give; then it is given to us LUKE.6:38.

4. Believe it is God's will to prosper you.

God's Blue print:

Malachi 3:10-11 are the blessings for tithing.
Mark 10:29-30 Pledges a hundred-fold return to those who make sacrifices for the sake of Christ and the gospel.
Philippians 4:19 Promises that my God shall supply all your need according to His riches in glory by Christ Jesus.
III John 2 says beloved, I wish above all things that you prosper and be in health even as your soul prospers.

Elijah told the widow to make a cake for him first and then the cruse of oil and meal would not fail during famine.
Genesis 26 Isaac sowed in famine and received a hundred fold return.

Be specific in asking for what you need from the Lord.

A. If you need money, be specific about what you need and what you need it for.

B. If it's a place to live, ask God for the place that he desires you to have.

C. If it is repair on the car, refrigerator, etc. Ask God to guide you to the right repairman and give you favor with them.

D. If it's the salvation of a loved one, be specific who it is and where they live.

E. If it is a matter of your church, ask God specifically for what is needed.

F. Jesus said you have not because you ask not. You ask and receive not because you ask amiss.
We talked about one of the requirements for walking in your inheritance of prosperity, which is paying your tithe. (See Chapter 3 and Chapter 4)

Now another key is "Whatever you can see by faith you can have". (See Chapter 13)

By that I mean that the First thing is the Spirit of God will have to teach you, so you'll have to be open to Him and Hungry for the Word of God. Now once you are prepared then He will lead you into the revelation of divine prosperity as you seek Him.

Second
Nothing is received from God without you having faith for it. So get this understanding in you that not only are you Abraham's seed, but that Abraham is the Father of the faithful or of those who walk by faith.

WHY? Abraham walked by faith and was blessed by God as a result.

1. Prompted by faith, Abel brought God a better and more acceptable sacrifice than Cain, because of which it was testified of him that he was righteous-(that is) that he was upright and in right standing with God and God bore witness by accepting and acknowledging his gifts. And though he died, yet through (the incident) he is still speaking (Gen 4:3-10)

2. Because of faith Enoch was caught up and transferred to heaven, he did not die. For even before he was taken to heaven he received testimony (still on record) that he had pleased and been satisfactory to God.(Gen 5:21-24)

3. Prompted by faith Noah, being forewarned of God concerning events of which as yet there was no visible sign, took heed and diligently and reverently constructed and prepared an Ark for the deliverance of his own family. By this (his faith which relied on God) he passed judgment and sentence on the world's unbelief and became an heir and possessor of righteousness, (that relation of being right into which God puts the person who has faith). (Gen 6:13-22)

4. (Urged on) by faith Abraham when he was called, obeyed and went forth to a place which he was destined to receive as an inheritance; and he went, although he did not know or trouble his mind about where he was to go.

RESULT
But without faith it is impossible to please God and be satisfactory to Him. For whoever would come near to God must (necessarily) believe that God exists and that He is a rewarder of those who earnestly and diligently seek him (out).

THE TWO KEYS
So the two things that have to be in place for you to receive prosperity are

1. The revelation in your spirit that God wants you to prosper and that He has provided prosperity for you.

2. Faith to receive the prosperity that belongs to you.

To receive an inheritance in the natural, first you have to know that you're an heir. God's word says we are heirs of God and joint heirs with Christ.
(Ro. 8:16,)

Romans 8:17: says If children, then heirs; heirs of God, and joint heirs with Christ. We are heirs! We have a heritage left to us by Abraham, and it has been carried down through a biblical lineage. Throughout the bible, we see men and women of God who walked by faith and who were prosperous.

We who are in the Body of Christ are not Old Testament servants. We are sons (John 1:12; Galatians 4:6; 1John 3:1-2). Since God had pleasure in the prosperity of his servants- those people under the old covenant who were not born again- then how much more does He have pleasure in the prosperity of His sons?

Those people in the old covenant were just serving the Lord. I serve the Lord, but I am more than just a servant. I'm an heir! You're an heir, too, If you're born again (Galatians 4:7). God is trying to tell us through many witnesses in His Word that He wants you to be in a position where you can be blessed and be a blessing.

We need to be fully engulfed in God, not barely getting by financially. Spiritually we ought to be overflowing physically sound healed from the crown of our head to the soles of out feet, mentally stable.

We should be walking in this all the time, not getting Holy Ghost goose bumps from time to time, and getting overflow from some one else when they get blessed.

Sum it up with Hebrews 11:1

Now faith is the assurance (the confirmation, the title-deed) of the things (we) hope for, being the proof of things (we) do not see and the conviction of their reality-faith perceiving as real fact what is not revealed to the senses.

God is saying to His people: this is what I want you to do: Bring all your tithes and offerings into my storehouse and there will be resources in my house.

God does not need our tithes and offerings. He is not hungry or without raiment. He does not want our money for Himself. He wants it for only one reason: so there will be resources available among His people-resources from which they can draw according to His riches

Phil 4:19 (AMP) And my God will liberally supply (fill to the full) your every need according to His riches in glory in Christ Jesus.

"You bring in your tithes and offerings". Then I will have a storehouse of resources from which you can draw your supply.

In addition to that, I will open the windows of heaven which you have shut up against yourself. I will walk in, take your disobedience, and fling it aside.

Then I will roll open the windows of heaven and pour (The American heritage defines pour as to flow or cause to flow in a steady stream flood) through them upon you a blessing that you will not even know what to do with it. I will give to you from what I own, and I own the heavens and the earth.

Gal 6:7-9 (AMP) Do not be deceived and deluded and misled; God will not allow Himself to be sneered at-scorned, disdained or mocked (by mere pretensions or professions, or His precepts being set aside), He inevitably deludes himself who attempts to delude God. For whatever a man sows, that and that only is what he will reap.

8. For he who sows to his own flesh (lower nature, sensuality) will from the flesh reap. I ask what will I reap and the answer is decay and ruin and destruction; but he who sows to the Spirit will from the Spirit reap life eternal.

9. And let us not lose heart and grow weary and faint in acting nobly and doing right, for in due time and at the appointed season we shall reap, if we do not loosen and relax our courage and faint.
I will paraphrase what I just said....God says: You sow it, I will grow it: and you will reap it "all in due season"

Haggai 2:8 "The silver is mine and the gold is mine saith the Lord of hosts."

The world needs to see Christians with the glory of the Lord shinning on their faces, with a shout in their souls and victory in their lives, because they are releasing their faith to God and He is meeting need after need in their lives.

This will burst your bubble; It is a crime not to live in seed – faith and let the devil's crowd have control of the wealth of God's earth!

I will tell you something else...All our health is not coming miraculously. Much of our health is potentially from several areas:

Our own body's healing properties, the chemicals of God's earth which He enables skilled physicians to administer.
Proper exercising of our bodies, right thinking and believing with our minds, prayer of faith available to us here on earth, and most important, we must recognize that God is our Source of the natural.

Also, all our spiritual help does not flow out of heaven. God has put His churches here on earth and has promised that where two or three are gathered together in His name, "I am in the midst of them" Matt 18:20

Where did the word prosperity come from?
It came from God

Where did the word success come from?
It came from God

Dorothy Ray has an awesome book (How To Be Successful In Life)
Go to Dorothy Ray International Ministries, Inc. (www.driminc.org) e-mail them for this book
(ISBN# 1-892304-13-9).

I have come to know that My God is the most high, he is the possessor of the heavens and the earth. He is the deliverer from all my enemies. He intends for his people to be prosperous and have good success, but if you don't know who you are in Christ Jesus or what your authority is in Christ Jesus, then you can be neither prosperous nor successful.

Another thing, I bet the devil has stolen the prosperity and success that you should be enjoying to the fullest and only because you allowed him to do it.

You know when we recognize who the thief is we can command him to return to us seven fold all he has stolen. Proverbs 6:31 (AMP) But if he is found out, he must restore seven times (what he stole); he must give the whole substance of his house (if necessary-to meet his fine).

People run around trying to meet important people, and they would give anything if they could just get close enough to shake the hand of a V.I.P. They hold up the names of people like the President of the United States, but guess what? His name is not above the name of our savior.

In Ephesians 1:20-22 Philippians 2:6-11. God has given Jesus a name that is above every name and above everything that is named in this world. Also, he says that all things have been put under Jesus' feet ....All things you name it.

Sin	Jesus name is above it
Fear	Jesus name is above it
Cancer	Jesus name is above it
Diseases	Jesus name is above it
Financial	Jesus name is above it

We have just allowed the devil to steal from us because we have forgotten who our God is and who we are, and failed to give our tithes as seed faith to him.

I will make a statement...
People who do not know who God is are without identity. They do not know who or what they are, and they can be neither prosperous nor successful in the ways God has provided for them. Why you ask? Because they allow themselves to be defeated by the devil and stay tormented throughout their lives.

It is by knowing God and knowing who He is that shows you who you are. When you know God, you become somebody, you take on the identity of God, your Father; Jesus Christ, your Savior; the Holy Spirit, your comforter; the children of God, your brothers and sisters; and heaven, your eternal home.

The new understanding that the Holy Spirit indwells us and enables us to pray both with the spirit (in tongues), and with the understanding
 (I Corinthians 14:15) is bringing us back to that intimate knowledge of knowing who God is.

Once we know that God is the most high. Possessor of the heavens and the earth, that we are heirs to the kingdom of God and that he owns the heavens and the earth. When we know this and have the revelation then we can know how god commands the right things for us.
He commands this earth to give up its riches.

He commands the windows of heaven to open up to us.
But the key is …we must choose to believe it so that when we give, we open ourselves up to receive.

God moves in our midst to deliver us:
To set us free
To make us whole
To deliver us from all the shackles and bondages and fears and sickness, financial needs

They put stripes on his back for your healing.
The blood coming from those stripes on His back is for our healing, and redemption.

We need to walk in a circle around the cross,
Not just stand in front of it for your or their soul's salvation (whom you have been praying for), while in front of it we receive His sacrifice for our sins being washed away. While behind it, we accept healing for our bodies.

Lay claim to what is yours.
Speak to the mountain in your life and tell it to go. In Matt 17:20 Jesus says when you make your faith as a seed you sow then you are to speak to your mountain of need. Tell it to be removed. The mountain will obey you and be removed! Then Jesus says, and nothing shall be impossible unto you.

So as the redeemed of the most high, it is high time for you to use the name of Jesus and command the devil to take his hands off God's property. That's you! You have ministering angels (the heavenly hosts), whose purpose in the world is to minister for you (Heb 1:14). You can release your faith for Jesus to send your angel on a mission of deliverance on your behalf. Your angel can take from the devil's hand what the devil stole from you, then bring it back and put it in your hands again.

So you need to open your spiritual eyes to what your God-appointed angel can do for you right here on earth.

God is saying to His people: This is what I want you to do: Bring all your tithes and offerings into My storehouse and there will be resources in My house"

Phil 4:19.And my God will liberally supply (fill to the full) your every need according to His riches in glory in Christ Jesus.

Something is a gift when the giver requires nothing in return. It maybe financial, material, service of one's talent and time, counsel and so on. It's something that will contribute to the well-being of someone or group at the expense of the giver's input. Through the gifts, God says he is moved to throw open the floodgates of heaven to bless the giver. It may not be instant or come in a way the giver may assume. However God works everything out in his way and timing to bless the giver.

Not only does he open doors for his blessings he also prevents the enemy from undoing our blessings. You may know people who received much only to loose it all in mysterious ways, to suffer crippling health problems or other misfortune. God works to prevent such experiences for as long as we continue obeying his word.

The world needs to see Christians with the glory of the Lord shinning on their faces, with a shout in their souls and victory in their lives, because they are releasing their faith to God and He is meeting need after need in their lives.

CHAPTER 8

Elijah The Tishbite

I Kings 17: 1-16

1. ELIJAH the Tishbite, of the temporary residents of Gilead, said to Ahab, as the Lord, the God of Israel lives, before Whom I stand, there shall not be dew or rain these years, but according to My word.
So in verse 1 we have a crisis, and a crisis is a signal for me to learn, and not lose.

2. And the word of the Lord came to him, saying,

3. Go from here and turn east, and hide yourself by the brook Cherith that is east of the Jordan.
It is not a sin to have a need in my life.
My need is an indication to change something in my life.
There is always a reason for my lack.

4. You shall drink of the brook, and I have commanded the ravens to feed you there.

5. So he did according to the word of the Lord; he went and dwelth by the brook Cherith, that is east of the Jordan.
There is always a special place for my blessing and supply from God.

6. And the ravens brought him bread and flesh in the morning and bread and flesh in the evening, and he drank from the brook.
God will always vary His methods of supply.

7. After a while the brook dried up, because there was no rain in the land.
God will sometimes remove our visible sources of supply to maintain our dependency on Him

8. And the word of the Lord came to him,

9. Arise, go to Zarephath, (meaning refinement), which belongs to Sidon, and dwell there. Behold, I have commanded a widow there to provide for you. God sometimes uses the illogical and the unlikely to supply my needs.

10. So he arose and went to Zarephath. When he came to the gate of the city, behold, a widow was there gathering sticks. He called to her, bring me a little water in a vessel that I may drink.
I rarely use my faith unless someone makes a demand upon it.

11. As she was going to get it, he called to her and said, "bring me a morsel of bread in your hand",
It is the responsibility of the men of God to make a demand upon it.
I must respect abundance enough to ask for it before it will come to me.
My faith will release the moment my mind focuses on a specific target.

12. And she said, As the Lord your God lives, I have not a loaf baked but only a handful of meal in the jar and a little oil in the bottle. See, I am gathering two sticks, that I may go in and bake it for me and my son that we may eat it, and die.
God will never ask me for something I do not have.

13. Elijah said to her, Fear not; go and do as you have said; but make me a little cake of it first and bring it to me, and afterward prepare for yourself and your son. God will always ask me for something I want to keep.
I already possess abundance in the form of a seed.

My supply for tomorrow can start with whatever is in my hand today.
God is aware of my present level of need.
Everyone has something to give.

14. For thus says the Lord, the God of Israel, "The jar of meal shall not waste away, or the bottle of oil. fail, until the day that the Lord sends rain on the earth".
The world's conditions do not control the Christians supply

15. She did as Elijah said; and she, and he, and her household ate many days.
My expectations affect my supply.
My consecutive giving creates a consecutive harvest.
God expects me to give with an expectation to receive
My reaction to a man of God in need determines how God will react to me when I am in need.
My supply depends on what I do

16. The jar of meal was not spent nor did the bottle of oil fail, according to the word which the Lord spoke by Elijah.
When I let go of what I have in my hand, God will let go of what is in His hand.

CHAPTER 9

God's Reward System

God's plan is through giving, sowing, planting.
Acts 20:35 Jesus said it is more blessed to give than to receive.

Gen 8:23 (AMP) Seedtime and harvest and cold and heat, and summer and winter, and day and night shall not cease. The farmer plants a crop and expects a harvest, but he has to sow, plant or give seed to the ground before it can reproduce, grow and supply a harvest.

Luke 6:38 Give and it shall be given unto you: good measure, pressed down, and shaken together, and running over, shall men give into your bosom. For with the same measure that you mete withal it shall be measured to you again.

Gal 3:7 Be not deceived: God is not mocked: for whatsoever a man soweth, that shall he also reap.
Tithing
Offerings
Alms Giving
Ministry
Vows
Labor
Penalty for Robbing God
100 fold return
Restoration
Take the harvest by force
Unexpected blessing (additional Promises)
Famine

1 Timothy 6:10: For the love of money is the root of evil: which while some coveted after, they have erred from the faith, and pierced themselves through with many sorrows.

It does not say money is the root of all evil, but the love of money is. People will lie, cheat, steal, rob, and kill for money.

Ecclesiastes 10:17-19: Blessed art thou, O Land, when thy king is the son of nobles, and thy princes eat in due season, for strength, and not for drunkenness! By much slothfulness the building decayeth: and through idleness of the hands the house droppeth through. A feast is made for laughter and wine maketh merry; but money answereth to all things.

Money is an earthly exchange, which is needed in every area of our life. It takes money for food, clothing, land, houses, cars, to pay utilities, taxes, insurance, etc. It takes money to keep our clothes clean, keep our houses and cars up, etc. We have to have money because it is the medium of exchange that is needed on earth. You may use a credit card or make a loan, but the lending agencies want their money.

On the other hand, there are people who have money, but they hoard it and live in poverty.

Here is a story about a person whose uncle by marriage lived in Seattle, Washington and whose brother lived in a large house, but lived in poverty. He ate out of garbage cans, lived like a beggar, but when he died and they went into his house, he had gunny sacks hanging all over the house. He was worth eight million dollars and who knows who got the money. One thing for certain is he didn't enjoy it or use it properly.

Poverty is a spiritual force that Satan sends against us. People who have a lot of money and hoard it have a poverty mentality. It is really called "the depression area" mentality. Many people lost everything they had during the depression in the thirties and they live in fear of not enough.

Poverty is more than absence of money. Webster says it is a poverty of the imagination. Those rich people imagined they were poor and lived like it.

Job 22:25 Yea, the almighty shall be thy defense (or covering or protection) and thou shalt have plenty of silver.

Ecclesiastes 7:12: For wisdom is a defense even as money is a defense but the Excellency of knowledge is that wisdom shields and preserves the life of him who has it.

Wisdom is a covering and money is a covering but the Excellency of knowledge will teach men how to spend their money wisely. God is not against us having money, as long as money doesn't have us.

3 John 2: Beloved I wish above all things that thou mayest prosper and be in health even as thy soul prospereth. That is total prosperity-we are a tri-part being. We need finances as well as a healthy spirit, soul and body.

All God is asking for is the tithe, 10% and you keep the 90%. Interest rates have gone up and prime rates have gone up, credit card rates, and everything else is sky high. Look at what happens if you don't pay Freddy Kilowatt (Edison) for using electricity, you will get disconnected and to restart service you will have to pay a deposit.

Now since the Garden of Eden, till now covers around 6000 years and God has never changed His interest. It is still 10%, and we get the benefit of the 10%. God even gives you an interest return – the windows of heaven blessings. You get the benefit coming and going. You can't lose, where else can you get this kind of deal. God wants you to be blessed, so you can be a blessing.

Revelation: God does not need your money, because he owns all the cattle on a thousand hills and all the silver and gold and He knows where it is at. So why mess with Him, when He put the gold in the rocks!

Tithing is a must: The tithe is the first tenth of your gross earnings, before anything is taken out. It is what you earn before taxes, insurance, house or car payment. You are to pay tithes. It is something you owe God.

The doctrine of tithing is found in Matthew 23:23: Woe unto you scribes and Pharisees, hypocrites: for ye pay tithe of mint and anise and cumin, and have omitted the weightier matters of the law, judgment, mercy, and faith: these ought ye to have done, and not to leave the other undone.

Most people will tell you that there is no mention of tithes in the New Testament because they think it was an Old Testament principle and does not apply to us.

The purpose of tithing is also to teach you to put God first in your life. God says if you tithe then He will pour you out the blessings until there is no more need.

Offerings:
An offering is what you give above the tithe, to meet the needs of others and to expect a return according to the size of your gift. When you give offerings you lay a foundation for God to bless you through others. Offerings are for future blessings.

2 Corinthians 9:7,10: Every man according as he purposeth in his heart, so let him give; not grudgingly, or of necessity: for God loveth a cheerful giver. He gives seed to the sower and bread to the eater and multiplies the seed sown.

Matthew 19:29: And every one that hath forsaken houses, or brethren, or sisters, or father or mother, or wife, or children, or lands, for my name's sake, shall receive a hundredfold, and shall inherit everlasting life.

We are to give offerings in good ground. It can be to missionaries, guest speakers, building fund, Christian television, ministries that feed you, the word of God.

The bible principle of economics starts with the tithe but are set in motion when we give offerings. There is a great blessing in offerings, because it determines the measure God will give back to you and it will bless the ministries receiving it, and supply their need.

2 Corinthians 9:8 God is able to make up to you by giving you everything you need and more, so that there will not only be enough for your own needs, but plenty left over to give joyfully to others.

Isaiah 32:20 Happy fortunate are you who cast your seed upon all waters (when the river overflows its banks; for the seed will sink into the mud and when the waters subside, the plant will spring up; you will find it after many days and reap an abundant harvest).

This scripture tells you not to give up on your seed if the hundredfold blessing has not manifested. You have to keep confessing and believing for it (after many days the plant will spring up and you will reap an abundant harvest). If Satan can get you to saying and believing the harvest will not come in he will steal your harvest.

Almsgiving:
Alms are acts of charity to the poor and unfortunate. Alms mean compassionateness (as exercised toward the poor). Alms can be given to the spiritually, mentally and physically poor as well as financially.

You don't pay alms, but you lend to the Lord, and God will repay multiplied.

Matthew 6:1-4: Take heed that ye do not your alms before men, to be seen of them: otherwise ye have no reward of your Father which is in heaven. Therefore when thou doest thine alms, do not sound a trumpet before thee as the hypocrites do in the synagogues and in the streets, that they may have glory of men. Verily I say unto you, they have their reward. But when thou doest alms, let not thy left hand know what thy right hand doeth: That thine alms may be in secret: and thy Father which seeth in secret himself shall reward (pay you for service rendered) you openly.

Luke 12:33 Sell that ye have and give alms; provide ourselves bags which wax not old, a treasure in the heavens that faileth not, where no thief approacheth, neither moth corrupteth.

A. Giving alms to the poor financially Proverbs 19:17: He that hath pity on the poor lendeth unto the Lord: and that which he hath given will he pay him again.

Proverbs 28:27: He that giveth to the poor lendeth unto the Lord: and that which he hath given will repay him again. God gets involved when you give to the poor and he is the only who will repay you.

B. Giving alms to the poor in spirit Proverbs 31:20. She stretcheth out her hand to the poor; yea, she reacheth forth her hands to the needy (beggar, destitute).

Matthew 5:33: Blessed are the poor in spirit for theirs is the kingdom of heaven. This means they are depressed in mind or circumstances, distressed in their human spirit, rational soul or mind. Most of them need to be transformed by the renewing of their mind in the word instead of looking at circumstances.

Dr. Cho told of how poor the people were in Korea when he started preaching, but now he has the largest church in the world and many rich people.

C. Giving the Word of God as alms:

Acts 12:24: The word of God grew and multiplied.

Mark 4:8,9: And other fell on good ground, and did yield fruit that sprang up and increased; and brought forth, some thirty, some sixty, and some a hundred. And he said unto them, He that hath ears to let him hear.

Luke 4:18: The Spirit of the Lord is upon me, because he hath anointed me to preach the gospel to the poor... The gospel to the poor is that they don't have to be poor any more financially, spiritually or physically.

Ministry:
God promises us that as we go out and win the lost that we can expect to receive wages.

John 4:36: And he that reapeth receiveth wages and gathereth fruit unto eternal life; that he that soweth and he that reapeth may rejoice together. Isaiah 23:18 Yet her profits and her earnings will be set apart for the Lord; they will not be stored up or hoarded. Her profits will go to those who live before the Lord, for abundant food and fine clothes.

Galatians 5:6: Those who are taught the word of God should help their teachers by paying them.

Vows:
A vow is a promise to God man or self. It is an oath covenant pledge contract agreement. Webster defines it as a solemn promise to God to perform some act or make some gift or

sacrifice.
A vow must be voluntary, an act of your will.

Numbers 30:2 If a man vow a vow unto the Lord, or swear an oath to bind his soul with a bond: he shall not break his word, he shall do all according to all that proceedeth out of his mouth.

Ecclesiastes 5:4,5 When thou vowest a vow unto God, defer not to pay it; for he hath no pleasure in fools: pay that which thou hast vowed. Better is it that thou shouldest not vow, than that thou shouldest vow and not pay. Suffer not thy mouth to cause thy flesh to sin; neither say thou before the angel, that it was an error: wherefore should God be angry at thy voice, and destroy the work of thine hands?

When you make a vow or oath or agreement with someone it is before God and he considers it a serious thing.

Job 22:21-28: Acquaint now thyself with him, and be at peace: thereby good shall come unto thee. Receive, I pray thee, the law from his mouth, and lay up his words in thine heart. If thou return to the Almighty, thou shalt be built up, thou shalt put away iniquity far from thy tabernacles. Then shalt thou lay up gold as dust and the gold of Ophir as the stones of the brooks. Yea, the Almighty shall be thy defense, and thou shalt have plenty of silver. For then shalt thou have thy delight in the Almighty, and shalt lift up thy face unto God. Thou shalt make thy prayer unto him, and he shall hear thee, and thou shalt pay thy vows. Thou shalt also decree a thing, and it shall be established unto thee: and the light shall shine upon thy ways.

God said he will supply all our need according to his riches in glory by Christ Jesus. When my husband and I made a vow to a building fund, God supplied all our need as long as he lived. That is why I believe God for the harvest of seeds sown that have not manifested. I made my prayer to him and I look to him only for my harvest.

Labor:
God says we are to rejoice in our labor. I was talking to a man today who is unemployed and he asked me to agree with him to get a good job. The place he was working closed shop and he said he doesn't like doing nothing and drawing unemployment

Ecclesiastes 5:19:Every man also to whom God hath given riches and wealth, and hath given him power to eat thereof, and to take his portion, and to rejoice in his labor: this is a gift of God.

Psalm 128:2: For thou shalt eat the labor of thine hands: happy shalt thou be, and it shall be well with thee.

Ecclesiastes 3:13: And also that every man should eat and drink, and enjoy the good of all his labor, it is the gift of God.

We are to thank and praise God for our jobs and rejoice and be happy when we have one.

Penalty:
The penalty for robbing God (not tithing) is 20%, Deuteronomy 26: 14 I have not eaten thereof in my morning (the tithe), neither have I taken away aught thereof for any unclean use (making the tithe unclean), nor given aught thereof for the dead (what God is saying is don't flush your money down the toilet by putting your tithe in a dead church where there is no anointing in them, no Word) but I have hearkened to the voice of the Lord my God, and have done according to all that thou hast commanded me.

The reason I share this with you is so you will get free by observing what I'm telling you. And I told you there is a 20% penalty when you don't tithe.

Leviticus 27: 30,31:(AMP). And all the tithe of the land, whether of the seed of the land or of the fruit of the tree is the Lord's, it is holy unto the Lord. And if a man will at all redeem aught (zero) of his tithes, he shall add thereto the fifth part (or 20%) thereof.

Let me paraphrase for you.
If a man has taken the tithe and used part of it for other things, in our society, you could be arrested for misappropriation of funds. So guess what, that is what you are doing with God's money.

Now God does not drops a rock out of the sky on you, but what happens is you get out from under the umbrella of God's protection and begin operating under the curse of the land, because you are robbing God of His tithe.

You just never seem to have enough money and what you do have is like putting it in a bag full of holes.

So verse 32 says again. And if a man will at all redeem aught (zero) of his tithes, he shall add thereof (to that which he redeems) the fifth part thereof. And that is 20%. So that means 10% plus 20%, or 30%. WOW I think it would be a lot better to give the 10% than to have to redeem it.

If you make $50.00 your tithe is $5.00 and you decide you can only give $2.50, you are short on your tithe $2.50. That is what you have stolen from God and that is what you have to make up. Because the tithe is the Lord's and the tithe is holy. You used God's money for other purposes. So if you want to stay in a position where your channels will continue to be open and God can bless you with the windows of heaven blessings, then you have to unclog the channel, by making up the $2.50 plus fifth part (20%). 50 cents, so you would pay back $3.00.

Deposits and With-drawls
Jesus told us that we have a heavenly bank account and that we should lay up treasures in heaven. There are only two basic ways to make deposits into the heavenly bank account; 1 is tithes and 2 is offerings or investing into the Gospel.

Now I will relate a testimony to you.

Benny Hinn told this. He said that when he was starting out in ministry, he hired a secretary who couldn't do much of anything and she was older and wouldn't draw stares. She was dependable and would show up everyday. He said that the ministry was small and there was a struggle with finances. This one minister was a thorn in his side and rubbed him the wrong way but God was dealing with him about tithing of all things. He said at the end of the month he got out the check book and told his secretary to write out checks to such and such ministry and so on, and God told him to write out his last $1000.00 dollars to this minister and her hand shook the whole time and he did too.

Well now Benny Hinn needed a miracle, he was almost broke, he had $2.10 in his pocket. He said that evening he went across town to visit a ministry and went in and was setting there when the Holy Spirit began talking to him. He said he put $2.00 in when the offering time came, and the Holy Spirit said Benny put the 10 cents in too. He said he looked around because he couldn't believe what he was hearing. The Holy Spirit said put the 10 cents in. He said Lord, all I have is 10 cents, I can't believe you want my last dime. The Holy Spirit sad Benny, put the 10 cents in. He said that he wrestled with the Lord over the dime and it was the hardest thing he ever did was to give his last dime.

He said the next day, it was looking like his ministry ended and the mail came. He said there were many checks that came in the mail including one with a letter from the minister who was a thorn to him, which said the Lord had me write you out a check for $10,000.00. He said for many weeks now money just kept coming in the mail.

I want you to know that you can't out give God and that God pays the biggest dividends.

100 Fold Return

Mark 10:30: says But he shall receive a hundred-fold return now in this time, houses, and brethren, and sisters, and mothers, and children, and lands, with persecutions; and in the world to come eternal life.

You will receive a hundredfold not after a while or not over there on the other side not in heaven not after you die not when Jesus comes back and establishes his kingdom but right now present tense now in this time in this life.

What will you receive? A hundred fold of what? Houses brethren sisters mothers children and lands.

Revelation:
There is a law of giving and receiving and there is a law of sowing and reaping. Give and it shall be given unto you or do not give and it will not be given unto you.

Reap the harvest
Did you know reaping your harvest is not automatic? Genesis 8:22: While the earth remaineth, seedtime harvest shall not cease.

You have to use faith on purpose to sow in faith, wait in faith for growing time by God an reap in faith to get the harvest.

Proverbs 10:5: (AMP) He that gathereth in summer is a wise son: but he that sleepeth in harvest is a son that causeth shame.

Ecclesiastes 11:4: (AMP) He that observeth the wind shall not sow; and he that regardeth the clouds shall not reap.

You can not sleep during harvest and you can not let circumstances keep you from reaping.

Mark 4:26-29: (AMP) And he said, "So is the kingdom of God is as if a man should cast seed into the ground; And should sleep, and rise night and day, and the seed should spring and grow up, he knoweth not how. For the earth bringeth forth fruit of herself first the blade, then the ear, after that the full corn in the ear. But when the fruit is brought forth immediately he putteth in the sickle, because the harvest is come.

1. Seed was sown in ground

2. Seed brought forth because God made it grow

3. Had to put sickle in (the sickle is a reaping hook). The one who sowed the seed had to reap the harvest.

It was not automatic.

The spirit of man is created to make faith grow, but you have to use your faith to do it according to the way God says it works.

Romans 3:26-28 ... but by the law of faith.

There is a law of faith about reaping as well as sowing.

John 4:34-36 says don't say there is yet four months to harvest. It is ready now.

Joel 3:13 Put ye in the sickle, for the harvest is ripe: come, get you down, for the press is full, the vats overflow...

Ye or you had to use the sickle. God didn't make it happen automatically. The sickle is symbolic of using the word of God over the devil. You use the word to get your harvest in whether it be for money you need or for ministry family souls etc. Matthew 11:12 The kingdom of heaven suffereth violence, and the violent take it by force.
We have to take our harvest by force.

I Timothy 6:12-17-19:(AMP). Fight the good fight of faith, lay hold on eternal life, whereunto thou art also called, and hast professed a good profession before many witnesses.

Charge them that are rich in this world, that they be not high-minded, nor trust in uncertain riches, but in the living God, who giveth us richly all things to enjoy. That they do good that they be rich in good works ready to distribute willing to communicate laying up in store for themselves a good foundation against the time to come that they may lay hold on eternal life.

We are to plant money into the kingdom as seed sown for our future. It doesn't say get rid of money, but don't trust in riches, but trust in the living God who gives us richly all things to enjoy. We are to be rich in good works, willing to communicate, and lay hold on eternal life.

We have to make a proper faith withdrawal just like withdrawing from a bank. John16:23:(AMP). And when the time comes, you will ask nothing of Me--you will need to ask Me no questions. I assure you, most solemnly I tell you, that My Father will grant you whatever you ask in My name (presenting all I Am).

Mark11:24:(AMP). For this reason I am telling you, whatsoever you ask for in prayer, believe -- trust and be confident – that it is granted to you , and you will (get it).

I John5:14,15:(AMP). And this is the confidence- the assurance the (privilege of') boldness-which we have in Him (we are sure) that if we ask anything (make any request) according to His will (in agreement with His own plan) he listens to and hears us. And if (since) we (positively) know that He listens to us in whatever we ask, we also know (with settled and absolute knowledge) that we have (granted us as our present possessions) the requests made of Him.

God said in each of these three passages that it is granted to us. It's a done deal as far as God is concerned when we are operating in faith.

You may say that I have been giving year after year and it hasn't come in yet. Don't pull on people to give it to you. But it is the Father who gives us wisdom supplies all things liberally and upbraideth not. Matthew 14:19; Mark 6:41; John 6:11 is the story of the lad with five loaves and two fishes, and the multitude that was fed. The lad sowed the five loaves and two fishes. He planted his seed in good ground.

Jesus took the loaves, looked up to heaven, blessed, and brake the loaves, and gave them to the disciples to set before the multitude: and the two fishes divided he among them all. He caused the seed to multiply. The harvest was enough food to feed approximately 15,000 men, women and children.

This was more than a hundredfold return. The increase was made by God. Jesus did not look to man, but he looked to heaven, to the Father, and blessed it then the Father multiplied the seed the lad had sown.

Ephesians3:20:God can do abundantly above all you ask or think according to the power that worketh in you. When you release your faith, the Holy Spirit can do the work.

Philippians4:19:says,"My God shall supply all your need, according to his riches in glory by Christ Jesus".

Don't limit God to what man thinks or can do or that you have to have money, but expect God to go beyond with a supernatural, miraculous supply to meet all your need.

When you plant your seed in your heavenly bank account as far as you can see its dead. It compares with when a person dies on earth his body is put in the ground, but his spirit is not in the body. The life of the seed is inside and it has to be planted in God's kingdom so the life that is inside the seed can multiply to produce more seed to the sower.

John12:24: I assure you, most solemnly I tell you, unless a grain of wheat falls into the earth and dies, it remains (just one grain: it never becomes more but lives) by itself alone. But if it dies, it produces many others and yields a rich harvest.

If you plant money then it doesn't reproduce, but when you plant your seed for multiplication, then it has to die before it can reproduce itself. That is why the harvest can not be instant. It needs time to grow. Sometimes God does give an instant harvest, but the norm would be in waiting for the seed to germinate grow and produce fruit for the harvest.

Now we can have more understanding in how God multiplies the harvest sown in our heavenly bank account. And the one thing he made me to understand that if is hasn't come in as quickly as we think it should, it means he is allowing it to continue to grow so that we will have a bigger harvest. It hasn't stopped growing by our time frame, but it is growing by God's time frame. He says in due season you will
Reap if you faint not.

Lets pray this prayer:
Father, I thank you that I have a heavenly bank account in heaven. I have made deposits and laid up treasures in my heavenly account. I break the curse that has been passed down from generation to generation of allowing Satan to steal our harvest. I have been planting my seed in good soil. I have been giving as I purpose in my heart -- not grudgingly or of necessity but willingly and cheerfully. My tithes and offerings belong to you Father. You said you give seed to the sower, and bread to the eater and multiply the seed sown, just like the lad with five loaves and two fishes I desire to have seed to meet my needs, to go and do the work of the ministry, and have seed to give to others wherever I go. I claim and lay hold on my harvest for I have put in the sickle and laid up treasures in my heavenly account and I believe you for the miracle increase in all I have given to date. You said when I give tithes and offerings you will rebuke the devourer over my ministry, family, employment, church and everything I possess or plant into, so I thank you for the supernatural increase now, because you do abundantly above all I ask or think. I ask you for the anointing to know how to disperse the harvest according to your will. Satan, I rebuke you over my harvest for His sake and the Gospel's. I am a thither and a giver. Devil I bind you on earth as you are bound in heaven. I cast you out of my financial harvest, Those tithes and offerings belong to God. I command you to take your hands off — my harvest and all the seed that I have ever sown because my seed is imperishable and God is still multiplying it for my harvest. I will see the miraculous increase in Jesus' Name.

Ministering spirits I charge you to go and bring in the supernatural harvest. Father, you said if I ask according to I John 5:14,15 that you have already granted me (my present possessions) the request made of You. I rejoice over my harvest, I bless it, and receive it now. It is mine. I give you thanksgiving and praise for the manifestation now in Jesus' — Name. Proverbs 10:22 says the blessings of the Lord it maketh rich and addeth no sorrow with it. Thank you for the miraculous, supernatural, abundant harvest that will come into manifestation now in this time Amen.

Remember natural seed is perishable, but supernatural seed is imperishable, If your seed has been planted a long time, keep your faith going until you receive the harvest.

TOTAL PROSPERITY: Proverbs 3:1-10 — Prosperity for the soul, verses 1,2

Social prosperity, verses 3,4

Spiritual prosperity, verses 5,6

Physical prosperity, verses 7,8

Financial prosperity, verses 9,10

CHAPTER 10

A Seed Sown In Faith Will Meet Any Need

Recession, inflation, and hard times have been with mankind since the beginning of time.

Gen 12:10: And there was a famine in the land: and Abram went down into Egypt to sojourn there; for the famine was grievous in the land.

At that time it showed that Abram was a coward and a deceiver. Because he was afraid that they would take Sarai his wife and kill him, he told Sarai to tell them she was his sister. But God told Pharaoh not to touch her because she was Abram's wife and it brought a plague on his house.

God had already told Abram that he would be great and would be blessed and his name would be great and that he would bless those who blessed him and curse those who cursed him, and all the families of the earth would be blessed.

Abram left Egypt rich.

The second famine is recorded in Gen 26:1-16 And there was a famine in the land, beside the first famine that was in the days of Abram...And the Lord appeared unto him, and said, Go not down into Egypt; dwell in the land which I shall tell thee of..

Isaac also was a coward and deceiver because Rebekah was beautiful and that they would kill him because of her. So he also told Rebekah to tell them that she was his sister. But Abimelech king of the Philistines called Isaac to him and asked if she was his wife and he said yes. Abimelech issued a decree that if any one touched her that he would be put to death.

Gen 26:1-16: Then Isaac sowed in that land, and received in the same year and received in the same year an hundredfold: and the Lord blessed him.

It goes on to tell how he became great and wealthy.

God told Abram to leave and go to another land, but he told Isaac to stay and sow. Ecclesiastes 11:4: says He that observeth the wind shall not sow; and he that regardeth the clouds shall not reap.

Psalm 33:18,19: Behold, the eye of the Lord is upon them that fear him, upon them that hope in his mercy; to deliver their soul from death, and to keep them alive in famine.

Amos 8:11: Behold, the days come, saith the Lord God, that I will send a famine in the land, not a famine of bread, nor a thirst for water, but of hearing the words of the Lord.

Luke 21:1-4: And he looked up, and saw the rich men casting their gifts into the treasury. And he saw also a certain poor widow casting in thither two mites. And he said, Of a truth I say unto you, that this poor widow hath cast in more than they all; For al these have of their abundance cast in unto the offerings of God: but she of her penury (poverty or need) hath cast in all the living that she had. This was a large sum of money to her because that was all she had, but Jesus was pleased with her and commended her to the disciples

The word of God is our guide to financial blessings, but the seed must be sown on good ground.

Isaac sowed his seed in famine, when everyone else was hoarding their seed or fleeing to Egypt.

The widow at Zarephath fed the man of God first from the last bit of meal and the meal did not fail and cruse of oil did not run out until the rain came.

The poor widow at the temple gave all of her living as an offering.

They all started at the point of their need, they planted seed, regardless of the circumstances, and they planted out of their lack or need.

You can get all you can and hold on to it or you can plant your seeds cheerfully, and help others and expect an abundant harvest.

Proverbs 11:24,25 There is that scattereth, and yet increaseth; and there is that withholdeth more than is meet, but it tendeth to poverty. The liberal soul shall be made fat: and he that waterth shall be watered also himself.

2 Chronicles 20:20: Believe in the Lord your God, so shall ye be established; believe his prophets, so shall ye prosper.

Statement
You have to be Godly and content and broke

That is a lie and doesn't line up with the word of God, But some of us are taught this, and so some of us say things like "I just want enough to get by" Boy are we living in a cave.

I Timothy 6:5: Perverse disputings of men of corrupt minds, and supposing that gain is godliness: from such withdraw thyself

What its talking about " He is conceited, understanding nothing, but has a morbid interest about controversies and disputes over words, from which come envy, strife, defamation, evil suspicions, constant irritations between men who are morally corrupt in thinking and the truth is not in them, who suppose that godliness is a means of financial profit."

So this verse is describing someone who would become covetous with money

Let's sum it up by saying it like this....
People with corrupt minds can't handle riches, because they won't do the right thing with money. Godly prosperity is talking about men and women with integrity.

I Timothy 6:6: But Paul goes on to explain something:
But godliness with contentment is great gain.

A person could be as godly and content without money as he could be with it. But he also could be more content with some money in his pocket!
Have you been content without money? I have served God with all my heart without a bit of it. But if we study his word, we find out we don't have to do without money.
I stayed content, and I stayed godly, but now I have added something to that---financial prosperity. I tell you, life is much better with prosperity than without it.

So if I'm going to be in this world, I might as well have a good life, not barely getting by, so I have added money to my godliness and my contentment, and guess what all three go well together, Godliness, contentment, money.

You see, when you have the Spirit of God and the Word of God inside of you, you can properly handle every dollar that comes to you. You become the master of money instead of money becoming the master of you.

Most of the people who are just after money in life are the folks who don't have it. And as I said, people who love money and who would become covetous with money will do anything to get it. They will scheme. They will break the law, and they will degrade themselves for money.

And Paul went on to say in I Timothy 6:7: For we brought nothing into this world, and it is certain we can carry nothing out.

So when you die, you know your family is not going to stuff your pockets with your money and bury you!
They only did that in Egypt for the great men and woman, and today when a tomb is uncovered in the pyramids, guess what the wealth is still there but there bodies have since gone. So I guess it did no good.

I'm not planning to take any money with me, but I'm planning to leave something for my seed because the Bible told me to do so. Proverbs 13:22: A good man leaveth an inheritance to his children's children.

How many times have you seen a car with a fish symbol on the window are bumper, and a sticker that says I'm spending my children's inheritance. Well guess this brings light to that thinking.

Here is some word to get in our spirit.
Deuteronomy 8:18..But thou shalt remember the Lord thy God: for it is he that giveth thee power to get wealth, that he may establish his covenant which he sware unto thy fathers, as it is this day.
God told Abraham, "I'll bless you and I'll make you a blessing"

Gen12:2…And when you're walking under the covenant, you'll be blessed, and you'll be a blessing.

God says that every thing I set my hands to do shall be successful if I line up in his word and his word abides in me.
God says he made me the head and not the tail
God says he made me above and not beneath
God says he will bless me coming in and going out.

So we can sum it up by saying:
God blesses us so we can support His Kingdom.
God reigns and rules over this earth.
He promotes His eternal plan.

God put money in the children of Israel's hands. He couldn't ask them for an offering unless He provided something for them to give.
It's the same today. He puts money in our hands then asks us for not only our tithes, but for an offering as well.
Our tithes and offerings bless His work.
When we bless His work, we can't help but be blessed
So I know that tithing helps me with the part of the covenant package that brings health and wealth.

Happiness comes from external circumstances or situations. We are happy based on what we receive into our five senses.

An example: if some one gives you $50.00 you're happy.
You receive a promotion, you're happy.
You get a job, you're happy. As long as our bodies feel well, we are happy.
The down side is, no one gives us any money, we are unhappy.
When we don't get the promotion, we are unhappy.
We lose the job we just got, we are unhappy.
We didn't get the new house or the loan wasn't approved, we are unhappy. All of these examples, feeling happy or unhappy depends on external stimuli.

But on the other hand let's define (JOY). Joy means regardless of what we see, feel, hear, taste, or smell, there is a word of God that enables us to give God praise at all times. Our strength does not come from happiness- for the joy of the Lord is our strength! If I say the Lord is my source of great pleasure that is because he is my total source.

Have there ever been times in your life that you wanted to just give up, I mean you just didn't hit bottom, you were below the bottom, you were under the barrel looking up, and all seemed that you would be better off dead.

But the joy of the Lord bubbling within prompted me to go on. To continue giving God praise clap your hands and continue standing on the word of God. So joy will bring you out, because you look to what the Word of God says and not what the circumstances or situations in your life determine.

I know what it feels like to have a loved one very ill. To go thru a time of extreme grief and suffering with a loved one where there has been a loss of not one but two lives in a six month period. Where I have went thru a devastating financial set back, no money, no food, no job, about to be set out on the street, my vehicle being repossessed, that it absolutely looked as thou there was no God who cared, but as strange as it seemed, joy of the Lord would bubble up and God would say You are where I can be your source now. This didn't make any since to me.

The word of God says, "When the wicked, even mine enemies, and foes, came upon me to eat my flesh, they stumbled and fell" (Ps. 27:2). We know the enemy wants to destroy us, but a joyful Word from within lets us know that Satan will not win. He has stumbled and fallen.

The thing we need to remember is that God is still God. We may not be able to fix every problem or situation but God is still God. As long as we continue to recognize God's sovereignty, we can make it. Often, testing's make Christians bitter instead of better, with no spiritual growth. It is not merely one's presence in such trials, but one's victory over them that brings spiritual growth and maturity.

The natural response to adversity is to escape it. But God uses trouble to mature His people.

We know that our trials are working for our good and we will still have a testimony of how the devil was defeated. James 1:3-4 says: knowing this, that the trying of our faith worketh patience.

But let patience have her perfect work, that ye may be perfect and entire, wanting nothing.

Let me make a statement:
Christians whom God can use the most are those whom God has bruised the most. The Word of God tells us that we will go thru trials and persecutions, or let me say it like this: With out Goliath's in our life, we would not grow in faith.

When we have confidence in God's word, all our needs are met.
1. Why are we whole, lacking nothing?
2. How can we say that after all we've been through, we still have the joy of the Lord.
Answer. Because the Word is in us and we know God will bless us with everything we need.

Okay I'm making another statement.
God cannot bless a double-minded person.

If any of us lack wisdom, let him ask of God that giveth to all men liberally, and unbraideth not; and it shall be given. But let us ask in faith, nothing wavering. For he that waverth is like a wave of the sea driven with the wind and tossed. For let not that man think he shall receive any thing of the Lord. A double minded man is unstable in all his ways. (James 1:5-8)

God wants to prosper us, but He cannot bless anyone who is double-minded. Double-minded people are unable to hold firmly onto their belief in the living God. The Word says, "For let not that man think that he shall receive any thing of the Lord". Either we believe in God, or we don't. Either we trust His word or we don't. A person who waivers back and forth might say, "I sort of believe in God" or "I believe God will do this, but I don't believe God will do that." Double minded people do not trust God's Word nor understand who He is.

John 15:7 (AMP) If you live in Me--abide vitally united to Me---and My words remain in you and continue to live in your hearts, ask whatever you will and it shall be done for you.

Have you ever heard the statement?
"What I don't know won't hurt me" or "What have I got to lose"

Let me tell you a truth
We get over 2000 ideas a day that pass through our minds, all we need to do is capture 1 good sound positive, God inspired idea and act on it to see it become a reality. God will give us creative, positive ideas, and if we act upon them according to his plan, they will successfully come to pass. Ideas come in the form of a hunch, a strong though that won't go away, intuition, or a knowing that you know. Ideas are like seeds, they must be sowed, cultivated, watered, pruned and developed, or they will not bear fruit.

1. Command to Abram: God said go for your self from your country.
From your relatives and your father's house to a land I will show you.

2. Promise To Abram From God:
I will make you a great nation
I will bless you.
I will make thy name great.
I will bless those who bless you
I will curse him who curseth thee.
In you shall all the families of the earth be blessed.
And I will make your descendants as the dust of the earth, then shall your descendants also be counted (Gen 13:16).

3. So what God is saying to Abraham "I am the God of more than enough".Gal 3:29 And if you be Christ's, then are ye Abraham's seed, and heirs according to the promise.

Don't forget God
God is your source of supply

God's promise (covenant) is that you will be blessed, so you can bless others.

4. Steps To Prosperity Or Keys

1. Decide What You Need. (James 1;7,8)
2. Lay Hold On It By Faith (Mark11:23,24) Husbands and Wife's Agree Matt 18:19.
3. Bind Satan's Power over what is yours
(Mark 16:17 James 4:7).
4. Loose the forces of heaven (Hebrews 1:14 Ps.103:20).
5. Never forget to praise him, in prayer for the answer.
6. Declare, say, and speak it as though it were already done.
7. Declare it as though it were already an accomplished fact.

THE LAWS OF HARVEST
A. Every harvest begins as a seed, we reap only what has been sown, (good or bad). While the earth remaineth, seedtime and harvest, and cold and heat, and summer and winter, and day and night shall not cease

B. You Must Render Your Seed Useless(Let it go don't dig it up)Verily, verily, I say unto you, Except a corn of wheat fall into the ground and die, it abideth alone: but if it die, it bringeth forth much fruit John 12:24.

C. Plant What You Expect To Harvest (Plant little get little, expand your vision, plant much)
And the earth brought forth grass, and herb yielding seed after his kind, and the tree yielding fruit, whose seed was in itself, after his kind: and God saw that it was good. Gen 1:12.

D. When Your Seed Is Sown You have Determined Your Harvest Size! But this I say, He which soweth sparingly shall reap also sparingly; and he which soweth bountifully shall reap also bountifully. 2 Corinthians 9:6.

E. Plant Your Seed In Good Ground.
But other fell into good ground, and brought forth fruit, some an hundredfold, some sixtyfold, some thirtyfold. Matt 13:8.

F. Planting And Harvesting Has A Wait Time Between
And he said, so is the kingdom of God, as if a man should cast seed into the ground; and should sleep, and rise night and day, and the seed should spring and grow up, he knoweth not how. Mark 4:26,27.

G. A Proper Harvest Requires Maintenance
And some fell among thorns; and the thorns sprung up, and choked them: Matt 13:7.

H. You Always Sow To Your Harvest Size, Not From Your Harvest Size.
Then Isaac sowed in that land, and received in the same year a hundredfold: and the Lord blessed him. Gen 26:12.

I. Your Expense Is Always More Costly At Harvest Time
FOR THE kingdom of heaven is like unto a man that is an householder, which went out early in the morning to hire laborers into his vineyard. Matt 20:1.

J. Part Of Your Harvest Is For Sowing Again.
Now he that ministereth seed to the sower both minister bread for your food, and multiply your seed sown, and increase the fruits of your righteousness; 2 Corinthians 9:10.

What we have just learned is that we reap much that we did not sow we reap the same in kind as we sow, since everything reproduces after its kind. There is a waiting period, because we reap in a different season than when we sow. The harvest never comes immediately, yet it will come, and we will all reap what we sow. But there is a kicker, we reap more than we sow.

When we put God first in our Tithe, God is faithful to bless those who put Him first. And He will forgive those who have failed to put Him first place in the past.

The Devourer has a right to bring destruction and famine in your life, when you keep what belongs to God and deny the provisions and protection of Lordship that is the curse.

The curse is called disobedience and provides the open door for demonic destruction. In this situation, at the end of your life, you won't even have enough money left over to cover the cost of burial expenses.

Question: What did you do with the money you controlled?
Question: Where did it go?

Haggai 1:6 (AMP) You have sown much, but you have reaped little; you eat, but you do not have enough; you drink, but you do not have your fill; you clothe yourselves, but no one is warm; and he who earns wages has earned them to put them in a bag with holes in it.

This is the scenario: Many Christians everywhere are doing without needed provisions. Out of ignorance, they are setting a place at their table for the devourer. Jesus is the Head of the Church, and should be embraced as the Head of your table. Put Him first and there will be more than enough to go around.

When we disobey and rob God of His place, we bind His hands. He cannot defend us against the destroyer or devourer when we have withheld the first things.

Question: Could it be that this is the same spirit that was released in Egypt? (Means Worldly)
Question: What happened with the plagues?

The Bible says that God gave the Israelites a way to distinguish themselves from the Egyptians.

God allowed the destroyer the right to enter the home of anyone who did not comply with His command.

Here is a key of Revelation: The destroyer respects nothing but the blood of the Lamb. God said "If the blood is on your door post, when the destroyer comes, he will pass over your house and your firstborn and all that you have will live.

Question: Can you imagine how much money is wasted in the lives of believers as a result of the curses at work in our lives?

But when we put Him first, He reverses the curse of the devourer and rebukes him for our sake, Because He is Lord.

Malachi 3:11 Amplified... And I will rebuke the devourer (inspects, plagues) for your sakes, and he shall not destroy the fruits of your ground; neither shall your vine drop its fruit before the time in the field, says the Lord of Host.

Terry's paraphrase of Mal 3:11:
And I will rebuke the devourer; anything that would consume, waste, destroy, gorge, swallow up, chew, prey upon you.

Such as the palmer worm (the gnawer=which means to bite on persistently, to wear away, to torment by constant annoyance).

Locust (the swarmer to fly off in a swarm, to move about or congregate in great numbers).

Cankerworm (the devourer to consume destructively; demolish) anything that comes in to devourer everything you own or posses.

Your treasuries...deposits in the bank, savings accounts, investments, etc.

Your life...your health...your family...your marriage.. your home...your ministry..

Your job…everything you possess.

God is saying he will make us plenteous in goods, in the fruit of our body, and in the fruit of our cattle, and in the fruit of ground.

Because we put God first and are a cheerful giver.
2 Corinthians 9:7 God loves a cheerful giver.

Let me tell you a story a Pastor told.
Conrad Hilton's heart was in the hotel business. He wanted to own a little hotel. Before long, he got one in San Antonio, Texas; then, he bought one in El Paso. Finally, he added another in Wichita Falls. He had three hotels when the Great Depression came, and he lost them all.

He went to work for a man in Galveston who assumed his notes on the land. Hilton prayed every morning, no matter how late he had worked the night before. In his book, he tells about going to his church and spending at least an hour in the presence of God each morning.

At the bottom of his despair, after he had lost all of his hotels, he saw a newspaper story about the grand opening of the Waldorf Astoria Hotel in New York City. He cut out the picture and wrote across it, The Greatest of Them All! Some day I will own it!

Now he was broke and bankrupt, yet he put the picture of this multi-million dollar hotel under the glass of his desk. Every day, although it looked like the end of the world had come, he saw that big picture of the great hotel, the Waldorf Astoria, the greatest of them all.
Supernaturally, he got his original hotels back; then, fifteen years later, he bought the Waldorf Astoria.

Later, the American government had him open the first international hotel. It became the largest chain of hotels in the world at that time, and He built it on his knees before God.

Hilton tried to train others to do it. They would come to him frustrated, saying, "How can you make it?" He would teach them his principles: prayer, faith, and hard work. Then it dawned on him, they were trying to make it on only prayer, faith, and hard work; it wasn't working for them because a key ingredient was missing. It was called a vision. He had a vision of "the greatest of them all." His heart was in hotels, and that is where his billions of dollars came from.

He knew that a vision, prayer, faith, and hard work would make him one of the greatest innkeepers in the world. Where his heart was, that's where his treasure was.

Let me now encourage you to say this prayer for prosperity:
Satan, I bind you and the spirit of mammon, greed, lust of money, love of money, covetousness of others money, idolatry of money, chronic indebtedness, chronic and excessive spending, wastefulness in my life. The Bible says the love of money is the root of all evil, but money is a necessary earthly commodity and Satan you will not hinder money coming to me to be used in the work of the kingdom of God.

Father, you said that you teach us to profit and lead us in the way that we shall go and that we are to eat the riches of the Gentiles, and in their glory or wealth we shall count ourselves fortunate. You said that you give us supernatural power to get wealth to establish your covenant, so we expect a miracle harvest because you get pleasure in our prosperity.

Father, you said that we are to cast our bread upon the waters and that we shall find it after many days. And we are to give a portion to seven and eight, and as we give to others you said to us shall be given, full measure, pressed down, shaken together and running over shall men give to our bosom.

Father, you said wealth and riches shall be in our house. You are exalted as head over all of us, you reign over us and both riches and honor come of thee. In thine hand is power and might; and in thine hand it is to make great, and you give strength unto all.

Father, you said if I obey and serve You, I shall spend my days in prosperity and my years in pleasures. And if I meditate on the Word day and night that I would be like a tree planted by the rivers of water, I would bring forth fruit in its season, my leaf or life would not wither and whatever I do would be prosperous and successful.

Father, you said if I honor you with my riches, and my tithe that my barns will be filled with plenty and my presses will burst out with new wine. You also said if I am willing and obedient I shall eat of the good of the land and you will supply all my need according to your riches in glory by Christ Jesus.

Father, I have planted seed in fertile soil, and I ask you to germinate it, reproduce it abundantly, so there will be an abundant harvest. Jesus came that we might have life and have it more abundantly (superabundant, excessive, beyond measure) and he became poor that we might become rich or prosperous by having enough to meet our needs and money to give to others to carry the gospel to the ends of the earth.

Father, your Word says what shall I render unto the Lord for all his benefits toward me? I will take the cup of salvation (prosperity, health, freedom from sin, deliverance from evil) and call upon the name of the Lord. I will pay my vows unto the Lord now in the presence of all his people. And I thank you, praise you, worship you and receive prosperity now in the mighty name of Jesus according to your word. Thank you Father for being so good.

CHAPTER 11

Claiming Your Rights As An Heir Of God

Christians have a heritage in Christ and many of us have not tapped into it.
Many of us have not honored our heritage of prosperity because we have failed to receive what God has provided for us.

Question: Are you a son or daughter of God?
Question: Do you think God is broke?

Answer: Not only is God not broke but he has given his children-a heritage of prosperity that can cause their struggling days to be over. Their days of lack can end

Romans 8:16,17: The Spirit itself beareth witness with our spirit, that we are children of God: And if children, then heirs; heirs of God, and joint-heirs with Christ; if so be that we suffer with him, that we may be also glorified together.

This means that what Christ has is ours,
But we have to walk upright,
We have to receive our rights,
We have to claim them by faith. And that comes by being taught the word of God and confessing the word of God.

Satan will try to hold back your blessings; by letting you walk upright but be broke. But when you know what belongs to you, and you are walking up right "You can say to Satan! I know you are trying to hold back prosperity from me, but I've come to get my goods in Jesus Name".

Let's look at the story of the prodigal son who claimed his inheritance but wasn't walking uprightly at first.
(LUKE 15:11-20).

And he said, a certain man had two sons; and the younger of them said to his father, Father, give me the portion of goods that falleth to me. And he divided unto them his living. And not many days after the younger son gathered all together, and took his journey into a far country, and there wasted his substance with riotous living.

Something Happens
And when he had spent all,
There arose a mighty famine in that land;
And he began to be in want.
And he went and joined himself to a citizen of that country;
And he sent him into his fields to feed swine.
And he would gladly have filled his belly with the husks that the swine did eat: and no man gave unto him. And when he came to himself, he said, How many hired servants of my father's have bread enough and to spare, and I perish with hunger! I will arise and go to my father, and will say unto him, Father, I have sinned against heaven, and before thee, and am no more worthy to be called thy son: make me as one of thy servants. And he arose, and came to his father. But when he was yet a great way off, his father saw him, and had compassion, and ran, and fell on his neck, and kissed him.

All of us have sinned and missed it in some way. We have all done something wrong in our lives at one time or another, and still do, but thank God that we can repent.

These younger sons said to his father, Father, give me the portion of goods that falleth to me.

And he divided unto them his living (Luke 15;12) Then it says, Not many days after the younger son gathered all together, and took his journey into a far country, and there wasted his substance with riotous living (verse 13)

Verse 14 and 15 says, And when he had spent all, there arose a mighty famine in that land; and he began to be in want.
And he went and joined (glued) himself upon one of the citizens of that country who sent him into his fields to feed swine.(HOGS.)

Some Christians are perishing because they don't want to go by the Father's rules. That's why the boy left-he didn't want to go by his father's rules. He didn't want to take any orders or be in submission to any authority.

You see some Christians are feeding swine, so to speak. But they won't pay their tithes, so they have to get money any way they can.

Verse 16: And no man gave unto him

Verse 17: And when he came to himself, he said, How many hired servants of my fathers have bread enough and to spare, and I perish with hunger!
That boy repented!

You have heard the truth about tithing and giving offerings but are still not doing it you're just like the prodigal son.

You say to the Father, "Help me. I want what's mine." Then, when the Father blesses you, you head for the good times.

You are like a prodigal son if you're not in the will of God financially. You've gone Away from home, so to speak.

Every time you get your check, you're getting some of your share, but you've cut yourself off from the Lord's ability to increase you, because you take that check and go out to the pig pin!

There are a lot of Christians enjoying their riotous living, throwing God's money away on cigarettes and booze, but they won't tithe. They need to repent for their riotous living and for robbing God! They've been robbing Him of the good pleasure of blessing them in the way He wants to bless them.

Luke 15: This boy had enough sense to repent. And, you know, if you'll repent, the Father will welcome you back into the house. If you haven't been tithing, just say, "Father, I've been stealing your money. But I see the truth, and I'm sorry for my sin.

You see you have to humble yourself like the prodigal son did when he "came to himself" while feeding those swine. You can't be as a little child if you are not teachable. Your spirit has to receive this revelation of divine prosperity

Luke 15:17: And when he came to himself, he said, How many hired servants of my fathers have bread enough and to spare, and I perish with hunger!

Verse 20.. And he arose, and came to his father. But when he was yet a great way off, his father saw him, and had compassion, and ran and fell on his neck, and kissed him.

Notice the son was trying to get his confession out: "Father, I have sinned against heaven, and in your sight, and am no more worthy to be called your son. "But the father was busy saying to his servants, BRING forth the best robe, and put it on him, and put a ring on his hand and shoes on his feet Verse 22

This is how the Father thinks about us! He wants us to have the best: Verse 23: And bring hither the fatted calf, and kill it; and let us eat, and be merry.

Let's read a little more, and learn about the elder son in connection with prosperity.

Now his elder son was in the field; and as he came and drew nigh to the house, he heard music and dancing. And he called out one of the servants, and asked what these things meant. And he said unto him, Thy brother is come; and thy father hath killed the fatted calf, because he hath received him safe and sound.

Here comes the attitude problem: And he was angry, and would not go in; therefore came his father out, and entreated him. And he answering said to his father, Lo, these many years do I serve thee, neither transgressed I at any time thy commandment: and yet thou never gavest me a kid, that I might make merry with my friends: But as soon as thy son was come, which hath devoured thy living with harlots, thou hast killed for him the fatted calf. And he said unto him, Son, thou art ever with me, and all that I have is thine. It was meet that we should make merry, and be glad: for this thy brother was dead, and is alive again; and was lost, and is found. Luke 15:25-32.

People are always talking about the boy who left home, but the boy who stayed home was as unwise as his run away brother.

Verse 29 and 30: And he answering said to his father, Lo, these many years do I serve thee, neither transgressed I at any time thy commandment; and yet thou never gavest me a kid, that I might make merry with my friends. But as soon as this thy son was come, which hath devoured thy living with harlots, thou hast killed for him the fatted calf.

Verse 31: And he said unto, Son, thou art ever with me, and all that I have is thine.

God is saying to his sons and daughters,
You're in my kingdom.
You are always with me.
All things are yours.
All that I have belongs to you.
You're in the family, and you're an heir and a joint heir with Jesus.
No good thing will I with hold from you as you walk uprightly, so put a claim on what is yours. Lay hold of it.

CHAPTER 12

The Woman With The Alabaster Box Who Washed Jesus Feet With Her Tears.

This account is written in the Gospel of Luke and Matthew and is to help prove that a seed will meet any need. Luke 7:36, 37. One of the Pharisees asked Jesus to dine with him, and He went into the Pharisee's house and reclined at table,

37. And behold, a woman of the town, who was "an especially wicked sinner, when she learned that He was reclining at table in the Pharisee's house, brought an alabaster flask of ointment (perfume).

Now Mathew gives a better description of the ointment and in the alabaster box

Matthew 26; 6-9: Now when Jesus came back to Bethany and was in the house of Simon the leper,

7. A woman came up to Him with an alabaster flask of very precious perfume, and she poured it on His head as He reclined at table.

8. And when the disciples saw it they were indignant, saying, For what purpose is all this waste?

9. For this perfume might have been sold for a large sum, and the money given to the poor..

So whatever ointment was in the alabaster box, it was the real thing, it was very expensive. It wasn't cheap stuff.

Now lets examine some more of Luke 7;37-44;46.

37. And, behold, a woman in the city, which was a sinner, when she knew that Jesus sat at meat in the Pharisee's house, brought an alabaster box of ointment.

38. And stood at his feet behind him weeping, and began to wash his feet with tears, and did wipe them with the hairs of her head, and kissed his feet, and anointed them with the ointment,

39. Now when the Pharisee which had bidden him saw it, he spake within himself, saying, This man, if he were a prophet, would have known who and what manner of woman this is that toucheth him; for she is a sinner.

40. And Jesus answering said unto him, Simon, I have somewhat to say unto thee. And he said, Master, say on.

41. There was a certain creditor which had two debtors; the one owed five hundred pence, and the other fifty.

42. And when they had nothing to pay, he frankly forgave them both. Tell me therefore, which of them will love him most?

43. Simon answered and said, I suppose that he, to whom he forgave most. And he said unto him,
Thou hast rightly judged.

44. And he turned to the woman, and said unto Simon, Seest thou this woman? I entered into thine house, thou gavest me no water…

46. My head with oil thou didst not anoint: but this woman hath anointed my feet with ointment.

Amplified says Luke 46: You did not anoint My head with (cheap, ordinary) oil, but she has anointed My feet with (costly, rare) perfume.

So what Jesus said is this
1. The woman's giving was an act of faith.

2. This woman came with some precious ointment and began to wash the feet of Jesus. She brought expansive perfume and her need was met. Now guess what, HER need wasn't financial. HER need was to be forgiven.

3. She brought precious ointment-a seed of monetary value-and she walked out forgiven of her sins.

Other Bible examples:
Luke 19:1-8: about ZACCHAEUS the rich man.

Luke 7:6-8: about the centurion who Jesus said I have not found so great faith, no, not in Israel.
The Amplified says for he loves our nation and he built us our synagogue (at his own expense).
Verse5: This man was also wealthy. He had built the Jewish people a church with money out of his own pocket. He gave seed unto the children of Israel, and look at what happened as a result.
The Centurion believed that if Jesus would speak just the word, then his servant would be healed. Notice what put the man in position for his faith to work.

1. He gave a seed, but his need wasn't a financial need.
2. His need was for something other than money.
3. The need was for his servant to be healed
4. And his need was met because a seed will meet any need.

Philippians 4:19: God will supply all your needs according to his riches in Glory by Jesus Christ..

I Kings 10:1-3: about the Queen of SHEBA. She came to prove Solomon with hard questions. But notice she didn't just come to

Jerusalem; she came to Jerusalem with something. She came with a seed.

Luke 5:1-3: About Simon Peter. Simon and his men fished all night and caught nothing. That was before Peter's seed met his need. In verse 3 it says that Peter allowed Jesus the use of his fishing boat. After Jesus had used the boat, He did something for Peter in return. He told Peter to go out and cast his nets into the deep, even through Peter had been fishing all night long and caught nothing. When Peter obeyed Jesus and cast his net, he hauled in such a load of fish that his net broke!

What kind of need do you have?
You might have all kind of seed out there, planted, just believing for the financial return. Well keep on doing that, because you will get money. But don't limit God there. Yes, money cometh, but believe for healing too. Believe for favor too. Believe for the Husband or Wife too. Believe for the children too. So switch gears a little bit, because that seed is supernatural. It wasn't sown in the natural realm. It doesn't only produce after its own kind; it produces in every single area-- wherever you are willing to believe

For the god of this world likes to keep men blinded to the truth. For without a vision, people perish (Proverbs 29:18)

The devil wants to keep the church in darkness because when she comes out of the dark ages, she is going to be doing something.

A carpenter once said, "It sure takes a long time to drive a nail in the dark." The church won't ever get her job done as long as the devil keeps her blinded to the truth.

The world says, "Give a man a fish, but keep him dumb and ignorant. Don't let him develop the talents, skills, and abilities God has put inside him; because when he gets smart, then you won't have power over him.

God's system is to teach, develop, love, and encourage you to hear the word of faith so that it will ignite the desires God placed within you to be somebody. God put His abilities within you and gave you power to create wealth.

A good man out of the good treasure of the heart bringeth forth good things; and an evil man out of the evil treasure bringeth forth evil things. Matt 12:35

I want to tell you a story that was preached by a minister named Russell Cornwell and many have considered it to be one of the world's greatest sermons and have used it for the wisdom it contains.

The title of this sermon is "Acres of Diamonds"

A man had a farm, but it wasn't enough. He wanted to be rich with diamonds. He wanted to find great wealth, so he sold his farm to travel around the world in his quest for the great treasure he desired; but he later died a pauper.

In the meantime, the man who bought the farm was out by the creek one day. He happened to look down just as the sun caught something sparkling on the ground. He picked it up to discover that it was a beautiful diamond.

That one diamond turned out to be one of the most valuable diamonds ever discovered, and the farm became the world's most famous diamond mine.

The original owner was traveling all over the world searching for riches, but they were in his own backyard all the time-he just didn't know it.

People travel all over the world to find their place and purpose in life and to capture success, but all along it is inside them, like a seed waiting to be cultivated!

The bible calls it "a treasure in earthen vessels." God has placed inside you, your life, purpose, and everything for which you were created. I believe that purpose is going to last throughout eternity. It is already preprogrammed and predestinated inside you.

For whom he did foreknow, he also did predestinate to be conformed to the image of his son. Romans 8;29

Let's compare you to a computer.

When a computer is created, the maker puts in the motherboard a bios which contains a set of machine instructions that you cannot change. Next is the CPU which is like a small person, a big person, old person, or young person which determines the speed. Then we add a hard drive (mind) to this to store and retrieve information. And it is this information (wisdom) which changes our direction.

What it means is that you have been born of the incorruptible seed, Jesus Christ. You have already been predestinated for everything God has for you. Like a seed, your purpose has tremendous potential inside it.

For we are fellow workmen-joint promoters, laborers together (co-creators, co-makers) with and for God; you are God's garden and vineyard and field under cultivation; (you are) God's building. 1 Corinthians 3;9.

You are God's field under cultivation. God has deposited Himself inside your life. When God gave Eden to Adam, He said, "Multiply, replenish, and subdue the earth. Conquer it and bring it under subjection. Bring it under control by the exertion of your will". You see you are God's garden. You are God's vineyard. You have been given authority to bring your life under control with the authority of God.

Inside you are the treasures of God. Inside you is Jesus Christ, the Hope of Glory. He has been made unto you wisdom, righteousness, sanctification, and redemption. His wisdom gives you the ability to see things and supplies ideas and future directions. This treasure in your earthen vessel is called talent.

For the kingdom of heaven is as a man traveling into a far country who called his own servants, and delivered unto them his goods. Matt 25;14: This story is called the parable of the talents. To some, God gave five talents; to others two; and to some of you, one. He has deposited them according to each man's ability. You have the responsibility to cultivate, replenish, and subdue these talents; your power of choice and your will power will release these good things of yours into the earth.

What God is saying is He wants to help you locate your treasure. God wants you to know the mysteries of His kingdom. He wants to open your understanding and give you direction. It is not his will for you to walk in darkness; rather, he wants you to see the riches He has deposited within you.

That the God of our Lord Jesus Christ; the Father of glory, may give unto you the spirit of wisdom and revelation in the knowledge of him: The eyes of your understanding being enlightened; that ye may know what is the hope of his calling, and what the riches of the glory of his inheritance in the saints. Ephesians 1:17-18

For where your treasure is, there will your heart be also. Matt 6:21. Let me paraphrase it like this; "Where your heart is, there your treasure shall be also".

Question1. Where is your heart?
Question2. Is it to God First? next your family or church?
I ask you again where is your heart?
Question3. What are the things you interested in?
Question4. Are you interested in music, ministering, or loving the sheep?
Question5. What do you enjoy?
Question6. What are your talents?
I tell you-pick one of them and develop, cultivate, subdue, and bring it into something great for the glory of God!

Each one of us has a sweet place in life, our Jericho. There's a sweet treasure in you, but the walls of resentment, jealousy, unforgiveness, doubt and unbelief, lack, sickness, and disease keep you from seeing it; but like ancient Jericho, those walls can be shouted down and we can let go of those peanut ideas and not caught or bound by the devil any longer.

We have to be obedient to putting God first in all that we do including out tithing and giving.

CHAPTER 13

Whatever You Can See By faith, You Can Have

STATEMENT: Decide what you want

KEY: Whatever you see by faith, you can receive if you will believe and not doubt

Every time Abraham turned around, he was getting blessed. Finally, he and Lot, his nephew who had been living with him, had to separate their flocks because they were too numerous for the land. Therefore, they divided the land between them.

And the Lord said unto Abram, after that Lot was separated from him this is what the Lord said "Lift up now thine eyes, and look from the place where thou art northward, and southward, and eastward, and westward".

For all the land which thou seest, to thee will I give it, and to thy seed forever. Are we also the seed?

And I will make thy seed as the dust of the earth: so that if a man can number the dust of the earth, then shall thy seed also be numbered.

COMMAND: Arise walk through the land in the length of it and the breadth of it; for I will give it unto thee. GEN 13:14-17.

1. We are Abraham's seed.. So why should we have less cattle, silver, and gold than the world?

2. So don't look down at the ground and say, "Everything is bad for me"

3. COMMAND   God told Abraham, "Lift up Now thine eyes, and look Gen 13:14.

4. Every promise in the word of God can be yours, if you (ACTION..DO) believe and apply that promise to your life by faith.

REVELATION KNOWLEDGE: THE PROMISES OF GOD'S BLESSINGS ALL COME TO YOU BY FAITH

A. You receive salvation by faith
B. You receive healing by faith
C. You receive financial blessings by faith
D. Salvation means being saved, but it also means having solutions to every problem.

KEY whatever you see by faith, you can have if you will believe and not doubt. All you need is to have faith like a grain of mustard seed. (Matthew 17:20).   REVELATION KNOWLEDGE. ..Your faith is the seed of life.

ACTION DO
First you do the spiritual act (plant the seed), then it produces the natural supply. Just believe and have a little bit of faith, then you can have what you see.

REVELATION KNOWLEDGE
And Jesus answering saith unto them, Have faith in God. For verily I say unto you, That whosoever shall say unto this mountain, Be thou removed, and be thou cast into the sea; and shall not doubt in his heart, but shall believe that those things which he saith shall come to pass; he shall have whatsoever he saith.

Therefore I say unto you, what things soever ye desire, when you pray, believe that ye receive them, and ye shall have them. Mark 11:22-24.

A. Faith activates the promises of God in your life and releases God to work for you, (KEY) but faith has to be fed the word of God to keep it strong. Abraham was justified not by what he could do, but buy what he believed God would do when he acted in obedience.

The first thing the seed of faith does is to put down some roots, preparing a foundation to hold the stalk that is coming. The bigger stalk, the more roots that seed must put down and the longer the waiting period it takes for the whole thing to develop and build.

If you have attempted some things that did not turn out the way you thought, don't get discouraged. If you did not lose your faith, the Word is still growing in your life and will bring forth fruit.

The bible says that ALL the promises in Christ are yea and amen
(II Corinthians 1:20). This means that Jesus Christ is not one to say "yes" when He means "no". He always does exactly what He says. He carries out and fulfills all of God's promises, no matter how many of them there are.

COMMAND   God said to Abraham. "Lift up NOW thine eyes, and look." That is just like God saying to you, See, I have given it to you. See, I've prospered you. "Well Lord, I'm not sure you're prospering me," you say as you look around. God is not talking about looking with your natural eyes; He's talking about looking with your spiritual eyes.

KEY Unless you see your desire spiritually, you cannot believe it.

However, when you see something in the word of God with your spiritual eyes, then you can believe it. I'm talking about more than mental assent; I'm talking about seeing it in your spirit through eyes of faith.

When he was beyond the normal age of productivity, Abraham had a son (Isaac) because he believed God. Through the eyes of faith, he saw what God had told him

While we look not at the things which are seen, but at the things which are not seen; for the things which are seen are temporal; but the things which not seen are eternal. II Corinthians 4:18.

REVELATION KNOWLEDGE

Do not look at circumstances. Look at the things which are not seen in the natural, but only in the spirit. Look at the promises in God's Word. God's Word will direct you even when you cannot see anything with your natural eyes. When you see God's promises, you overcome the visible with the invisible. After you see the promise, you must go out and claim your possessions. You must have corresponding actions of faith, and this requires work. Laziness will never get you God's blessings or prosperity.

COMMAND   God told Abraham. "Arise, WALK through the land (Kingdom of God and His promises)". Gen 13:17.

ACTION DO He had to act on his faith to possess his inheritance. You will too. You will need to walk out your possessions and work out your inheritance.

When God tells you to walk out the land of your inheritance, He means it. If you are willing and obedient, you CAN:
Possess the land
Prosper
Have God's blessings
Possess the gates of every one of your enemies

Lets take a step back in to time.

A tithe is a charge on farm produce or labor that is used to maintain and support religious activities.
Abraham paid a tithe of the spoils of war to Melchizedek: Gen 14:20 (And blessed, praised and glorified be God Most High Who has given your foes into your hand! And (Abram) gave him a tenth of all (he had taken). Heb 7:1-10.

Story is about Melchizedek:

1. For this Melchizedek, king of Salem and Priest of the Most High God, met Abraham as he returned form the slaughter of the kings and blessed him;

2. And Abraham gave to him a tenth portion of all (the spoil). He is primarily, as his name when translated indicates, king of righteousness, and then he is also king of Salem, which means king of peace.

3. Without (record of) father or mother or ancestral line, nor with beginning of days or ending of life, but resembling the Son of God he continues to be a priest without interruption and without successor.

4. Now observe and consider how great (a personage) this was to whom even Abraham the patriarch gave a tenth the topmost (the pick) of the heap of the spoils.

5. And it is true that those descendants of Levi who are charged with the priestly Office are commanded in the Law to take tithes

from the people, which means from their brethren, though these have descended from Abraham.

6. But this person who has not their Levitical ancestry received tithes from Abraham (himself) and blessed him who possessed the promises (of God).

7. Yet it is the lesser person who is the blessed by the greater one.

8. Furthermore, here (in the Levitical priesthood) tithes are received by men who are subject to death; while there (in the case of Melchizedek), they are received by one of whom it is testified that he lives (perpetually).

9. A person might even say that through Abraham, Levi (the father of the priestly tribe) himself, who received tithes, paid tithes through Abraham.
For he was still in the loins of his forefather (Abraham) when Melchizedek met him (Abraham)

According to Deuteronomy 12:2-7, 17-19; 14:22-29
Terry's paraphrased for you. You shall destroy all the places where the nations you dispossess served their gods, upon the high mountains.
the hills.
under every green tree.
you shall break down their altars.
dash in pieces their pillars.
burn their Asherim with fire.
you shall hew down the graven images of their gods.
and destroy their name out of that place.
You shall not behave so toward the Lord your God.
But you shall seek the place which the Lord your God shall choose and you shall bring your burnt offerings your sacrifices

your tithes offering of your hands your vows your freewill offerings and the firstlings of your herd and of your flock.

And there you shall eat before the Lord your God, and you shall rejoice in all to which you put your hand, you and your households, in which the Lord your God has blessed you.

You may not eat within your towns the tithe of your grain or of your new wine or of your oil or the firstlings of your herd or flock, or anything you have vowed, or your freewill offerings, or the offerings from your hand (of garden products).18. But you shall eat them before the Lord your God in the place which the Lord your God shall choose, you and your son and your daughter, your manservant and your maidservant, and the Levite that is within your towns; and you shall rejoice before the Lord your God in all that you undertake.

Take heed not to forsake or neglect the Levite (God's minister) as long as you live in the land.

A quick history lesson is this.
Ashdod and Ashdodites were one of five principal cities of the Philistines. They were originally inhabited by the Anakim (giants) Josh 11:22; 13:3. Before the kingship of Saul, the philistines defeated the Israelites at Ebenezer: they captured the ark of the covenant and brought it to Ashdod, placing it in the temple dedicated to their god Dagon. Following this, the stone image of the god Dagon fell on its face and broke, and the Ashdodites suffered a plague. The terrified Philistines decided that the ark could not remain with them and sent it back to Israel

Now the Prophet Malachi (Malachi 3:8-10) boldly declared not paying tithes was robbing God., promised full barns and vats, opened windows of heaven, outpoured blessing, and deliverance from locusts, in return for faithful tithing. Providing for the temple and the priests in the service of God remained the chief purpose of tithing.

Now less come to where we are today.

New Testament:
Matthew 23:23: and Luke 11:42.. Mat 23:23.."How terrible it will be for you teachers of religious law and you Pharisees. Hypocrites! For you are careful to tithe even the tiniest part of your income (mint, dill, and cumin), but you ignore the important things of the law-justice, mercy, and faith. You should tithe, yes, but you should not leave undone the more important things.

Jesus pronounced how terrible it would be for the Pharisees because although they were keeping the tiniest details of law, ceremony, custom, and tradition, they were forgetting justice and the love of God. Jesus did not condemn the practice of tithing, even of small amounts if one chose to do so.

Jesus condemned the Pharisees for being scrupulous in less important matters while completely neglecting the larger issues that were far more important-such as dealing correctly and fairly with the people and building a relationship with God. And in verse 24 Jesus slams them. Blind guides! You strain your water so you won't accidentally swallow a gnat; then you swallow a camel! Jesus spoke of those who meticulously paid tithes on three small garden herbs while neglecting three weightier matters of the law, justice, mercy, and faith...This was an example of the lack of a right sense of priorities that marked the Pharisees. It is so much easier to feel self-satisfied by following explicit rules than it is to live with moral sensitivity in our relationships with God and others.

According to Luke 18:12: the Pharisee, congratulating himself in prayer for his superior virtues, mentions his tithing of all income among his claims to divine favor. Christ sternly denounced this man's prideful performance, valuing instead the humble, repentant person.

What are the Biblical purposes and principles behind tithing.

You must set aside a tithe of your crops-one tenth (What ever your crops may be.)

Bring this tithe to the place your God chooses for his name to be Honored.
The bible makes the purpose of tithing very clear-to put God first in our life.
We are to give God the first and the best of what we earn.
What we do first with our money shows what we value most.
Giving the first part of our paycheck to God immediately focuses our attention on him. It reminds us that all we have belongs to him.

A habit of regular tithing can keep God at the top of our priority list and give us a proper perspective on everything else we do.

The value of a gift is not determined by its amount, but by the spirit in which it is given. A gift given grudgingly or for recognition loses its value.
When you give, remember-no matter how small or large your income, your tithe is pleasing to God when it is given out of gratitude and a spirit of generosity.
So remember this Mark 12:41-44 Jesus watches what you put into the treasury.

Key 1 If you demand that the only things you allow to stick in your mind are those things that line up with the Word of God, you will find yourself not easily misguided by new doctrines which come from many sources around.

Revelation You will find yourself rising up out of your defeat or near-defeat, and moving into new bold adventures for your God.

2. Corinthians 10:5 Casting down imaginations, and every high thing that exalteth itself against the knowledge of God, and bringing into captivity every thought to the obedience of Christ.

Revelation If there is going to be transformation in any area of your life, your mind must be cleansed of the unscriptural principles and be reprogrammed to line up with God's original intentions in His precious Word.

Promise As your mind is renewed, you will become what God intended for you to be in the very beginning, when He planned for you to have victories and conquests as you serve Him.

He wants to break those old concepts which are set in concrete in your mind, and put His mind into you. Scripture encourages us to have the mind of Christ: Let this mind be in you, which was also in Christ Jesus. Phil 2:5 and then the scripture goes on to say in Ro 12:…And be not conformed to this world: but be ye transformed by the renewing of your mind, that ye may be prove what is that good and acceptable, and perfect, will of God.

Revelation
You see, until you become a great receiver, you will not be able to become a great giver, you will not be a great receiver.
Something has to change.
Something has to move.
The cycle has to be broken, and the abundance cycle must be started.

The thing that has to move is that old thinking process that continues to bring you to the insufficiency you have lived with for so long. Now let Jesus make all things new!

Revelation God does want you to prosper 3 John 2: Beloved, I wish (pray) above all things that thou mayest prosper and be health, even as thy soul prospereth.

When you come out of the cycle of lack you need to come into the cycle of abundance.
When you come out of the cycle of want you need to come into the cycle of more than enough.

Key. Your current financial condition is determined by your past obedience in giving

Key. Your future financial condition will be determined by your obedience today

Every time God tells you to give a certain amount, you must release the amount He tells you to give, whether it is given to your church, to a Christian telethon or to a great mission endeavor. God is not only raising money for the vision or outreach to which you are giving, He is also raising future money for you and the vision He plans for you to accomplish for Him.

Faith=Action If you start tithing and giving now there will be a little time of catching up to God's prosperity for your life. You did not get into your present situation in a day, so do not expect God to get you out of it in a day.

Revelation You never reap the same day you sow. It will take a season for your new prosperity crops to become ready for harvest.

The Bible says that if you sow, in due season, you will reap.

If you cast your bread on the water, in a number of days, it will come back to you again; God says the blessings will overtake you!

God's word is pregnant with promises of reaping the harvest if you are faithful in sowing.

Promise The bible speaks of a ministry a special grace for giving- so we can literally become God's bankers, those who will finance God's work with the money with which He has prospered us.

2 Corinthians 9:6,7,11: (Remember) this: he who sows sparing and grudgingly, will also reap sparing and grudgingly, and he who sows generously and that blessings may come to someone, will also reap generously and with blessings.

7. Let each one give as he has made up his own mind and purposed in his heart, not reluctantly or sorrowfully or under compulsion, for God loves (that is, He takes pleasure in, prizes above other things, and is unwilling to abandon or to do without) a cheerful (joyous, prompt-to-do-it) giver—whose heart is in giving.

Thus you will be enriched in all things and in every way, so that you can be generous, (and your generosity as it is) administered by us will bring forth thanksgiving to God.

CHAPTER 14

You And God Make An Un-Beatable Team

God created Adam and Eve and placed them in a garden of plenty. They were his companions. They shared his abundant living. It was his will that they enjoy.
Plenty of happiness and pleasure
Plenty of energy and strength
Plenty of peace and love
Plenty to eat and enjoy
Plenty of health and life
Plenty of everything
That is God's will for you today

Question.
1. Are you depressed?
2. Do you struggle to make ends meet?
3. Is there never enough money to pay your bills?
4. Are you plagued by sickness?
5. Do you worry and are you troubled?
6. Are you alone and insecure?
7. Are you burdened by problems you can't solve?
8. Have you done wrong to somebody?
9. Do you need to forgive anyone?
10. Have you found true happiness?
11. Are you at peace?
12. Are your goals clear?
13. Would you like greater prosperity?
14. Do you need a real friend-some one you can trust?
15. Do you need to help someone else?
16. Do you have any enemies?
17. Are you a winner?

I have already told you that God's will for you is to not want or lack, but to have plenty.

With all of your shortcomings or problems or disadvantages, God is still on your side. Faith even smaller than a grain of mustard seed will start a miracle in your life today!

The Garden of Eden shows you what God wants for you. You are about to discover the road that will lead you back to the paradise that was forfeited so long ago.

Perhaps you have made mistakes. There may be things you would do differently if you could start over.

Today you are here and it is not by accident. The Pastor will give you the opportunity today to make Jesus your Savior.

Jesus came so that we might have life more abundantly, and He shows us what God wants us to have.

Jesus opened the door to God's limitless mercy and abundance, through His death on the cross.

Every miracle he performed was an example of what God wills to do for every other person in similar circumstances.

When He met people burdened and tormented by sins, wrongs, evil and injustices which they had committed against themselves, against their neighbors and against God, He performed a spiritual miracle in their lives. HE FORGAVE THEM!

When Jesus encountered those who suffered with diseases and those who were crippled or paralyzed, HE MIRACULOUSLY CURED THEIR BODIES and restored them to health.

When Jesus found people in material need, Guess what he did, HE PROVIDED FOR THEM, even when it called for a material miracle.

In John 10:10- Jesus said the thief's purpose is to steal, kill and destroy, but I came to give you life in it's fullness

Webster's defines steal: to take another's property without permission or right. Satan has done this and still does it today by conditioning their minds to accept poverty, fear, sickness, and defeat and thru this negative process you have been cheated out of God's abundance.

I have already told you that God's will for you is to not want or lack, but to have plenty!

With all of your shortcomings or problems or disadvantages God is still on your side. Faith even smaller than a grain of mustard seed will start a miracle in your life today!

The Garden of Eden shows you what God wants for you. You are about to discover the road that will lead you back to the paradise that was forfeited so long ago. Perhaps you have made mistakes. There may be things you would do differently if you could start over. Today you are here and it is not by accident. The Pastor will give you the opportunity today to make Jesus your Savior, and be able to start over.

Jesus came so that we might have life more abundantly, and He shows us what God wants us to have. Jesus opened the door to God's limitless mercy and abundance, through His death on the cross.

Every miracle he performed was an example of what God wills to do for every other person in similar circumstances.

Webster's defines steal: to take another's property without permission or right. Satan has done this and still does it today by conditioning your minds to accept poverty, fear, sickness, defeat and thru this negative process you have been cheated out of God's abundance.

Webster's defines kill: to cause the death of; slay, to destroy; extinguish. Satan has been doing this and still does it today through disease and fear, want, distress, tension and failure.

Webster's defines destroy: to injure beyond repair; demolish, to put an end to, to make ineffective or useless, to kill. Satan has been doing this and still does it today through the plague of loneliness and poverty, of sickness and evil, of fear and problems has destroyed the influence and effectiveness, health and happiness of millions whom God intended for happiness and prosperity.

Look at what Jesus did for the people then and today he still wills the same for you and your house.

Jesus came to solve your problems, to forgive your sins, to heal your sicknesses, to give you success, to walk with you, to surround you with good things, to give you energy, to fill you with life and love and health.
Jesus came to
Solve your problems,
To forgive your sins,
To heal your sicknesses,
To give you success,
To walk with you,
To surround you with good things,
To give you energy,
To fill you with life and love and health.

Spiritually, God wills that you have peace, tranquility, faith, creativity and life and abundance.

Physically He offers healing, energy, a strong body and abundance of health.
He offers success, achievement, prosperity, abundance and success to the divine source of all of God's plenty.

Materially, He offers success, achievement, prosperity, abundance and success to the divine source of all of God's plenty

The bible clearly confirms God wants you to enjoy plenty and live in abundance.

You'll have to break your way out of that misconception-and you'll only do it if you are willing for God to bless and prosper you for His glory.

If you ever hope to accomplish anything for yourself, for others and for God, you will need to discover the miracle-source of God at work in man, and the wonderful purpose God has for you in this life. Discover your true value, your potential for happiness, health, success and prosperity with God.

You and God in you is a powerful driving force that you can learn to release to achieve miracles for yourself and for the good and happiness of others, but only if you learn to look in the right direction.

Key. What you imagine and what you talk about is what you become.

Revelation: Your thoughts and your words have the mysterious power of creating the situation that surrounds you. They are the seeds you sow and they reproduce of their kind.

Key. Get God's opinion of yourself
       Find your roots in Royalty
       Think of yourself as God thinks of you
       Talk of yourself as He doe's-in the bible

And when you do this, it starts the miraculous positive drive of His power inside of you. As His seeds of truth and faith are planted in you, they will produce God's kind of a person

The overwhelming majority took one look at that wealthy land, and fled. They said: it's too good to be true. This land of milk and honey can't be for us. Giants are there. We saw them. We felt like grasshoppers. They can destroy us. They thought that way. They talked that way and reaped that crop. They acted that way and never inherited the Plenty God purposed for them. They died in want.

Only two men looked at things like God saw them, and spoke like God. They said: This is a good land of plenty and since we are God's people, we can take it and enjoy it. So they inherited it. This was Joshua and Caleb. You see they knew the land of milk and honey belonged to royalty

This all starts with obedience that Jesus came so that we might have life more abundantly, and He shows us what God wants us to have. Jesus opened the door to God's limitless mercy and abundance, through His death on the cross.

Gen 28:16-22: Jacob awoke from his sleep, and said surely the Lord is in this place and I did not know it. Then he said this is none other than the house of God and this is the gateway to heaven. Then Jacob rose early in the morning and took the stone he had put under his head and he set it up for a pillar (a monument to the vision in his dream), and he poured oil on its top (in dedication).

Then he named that place Bethel (the house of God) Then he made a vow, saying If God will be with me and will keep me in this way that I go, and will give me food to eat and clothing to wear, so that I may come again to my father's house in peace, then the Lord shall be my God. And this stone, which I have set up as a pillar (monument), shall be God's house (a sacred place to me) and of all the increase of possessions) that you give me I will give the tenth to you.

If you ever hope to accomplish anything for yourself, for others and for God, you will need to discover the miracle-source of

God at work in man, and the wonderful purpose God has for you in this life.
Discover your true value, your potential for happiness, health, success and prosperity with God.

You and God in you is a powerful driving force that you can learn to release to achieve miracles for yourself and for the good and happiness of others, but only if you learn to look in the right direction.

Now that you have read this book:
If you haven't make Jesus Christ Lord and Savior, Then repeat this simple prayer:

Father, I come to you right now in the Name of Jesus.
I realize now that I really have never known you,
I choose now to ask you to come into my heart and forgive me of all my sins.
I choose to renounce my past and I choose to accept you as Lord and Savior.
I do believe in my heart that God raised Jesus from the dead and confessed it with my mouth that I would be saved.
Thank you for forgiving me, loving me, and making me accepted in the beloved.   Amen

PRAYER FOR MONEY TO COME IN

Satan, I bind you and the ruler prince of poverty, lack, depression era spirit, looting, arson, stealing, Judas Spirit of greed and thievery, fraud, extortion, forgery, stealing, kleptomania, robbing, grand theft, grand larceny and petty larceny, embezzlement, swindling, plundering, looting, burglary, smuggling, robbing spoils of public, ill-gotten gain over your name income, finances, and business ventures. I loose prosperity and hidden riches in secret places (Isaiah 45:3) to come from foreign banks, gangsters, mobsters, politicians, drug dealers, wealth of the sinner, prostitutes, pimps, illegal dealers of all kinds, stolen money of thieves, money from usury and unjust gain, money hidden in homes, ground, clothing, beds, vaults, lock boxes in savings and loans, banks, sweepstakes, lotteries, inheritances, business needing services, advertising, gifts, ideas, witty inventions, one hundredfold return from offerings, and land sales to be used by your name for buildings, equipment, personnel and skilled and cunning workmen to be used to get finances for the end-time global harvest to meet the needs of you and or who you are praying for.

Father, you said in Psalms 147:15 that He sendeth his commandment upon earth: his Word runneth very swiftly, and Hebrew 1:14 says Are they not all ministering spirits sent forth for us who are heirs of salvation? So we ask you Father to send forth your angels to the north, south, east and west to bring this word to pass very swiftly. We desire the swift provisions of money to finance the work you have called us to do. You said the blessings of the Lord they make us rich and add no sorrow to it. You also said we can decree a thing and it shall be established so we declare and decree that your Word is true and we call those riches to come in speedily to your name or who ever you are praying for in the Name of Jesus.

We cover your name or who ever you are praying for with the shed blood of the Lord Jesus to protect us, guide us and watch over us. The Word says we have overcome Satan by the blood of Jesus and the word of our testimony; and Satan you cannot cross the bloodline over anything your name operates, owns or possesses in Jesus Name.

Father we bring our offering according to Psalm 96:8,9 that says Give unto the Lord the glory due unto his name: bring an offering, and come into his courts. O worship the Lord in the beauty of holiness: fear before him, all the earth and we thank you, praise you and worship your name. You are the Almighty God who answers our prayers according to your word. We receive it now and thank you in Jesus Name.

Used with permission:
Prayer written by Dorothy Ray
Dorothy Ray International Ministry, Inc
www.driminc.org

www.ingramcontent.com/pod-product-compliance
Lightning Source LLC
LaVergne TN
LVHW051604070426
835507LV00021B/2755